We Believe

We Believe

Muslims and Christians in Conversation about Faith

Veli-Matti Kärkkäinen

CASCADE *Books* • Eugene, Oregon

WE BELIEVE
Muslims and Christians in Conversation about Faith

Cascade Books
An Imprint of Wipf and Stock Publishers
199 W. 8th Ave., Suite 3
Eugene, OR 97401

www.wipfandstock.com

PAPERBACK ISBN: 978-1-7252-7670-3
HARDCOVER ISBN: 978-1-7252-7671-0
EBOOK ISBN: 978-1-7252-7672-7

Cataloguing-in-Publication data:

Names: Kärkkäinen, Veli-Matti, author.

Title: We believe : Muslims and Christians in conversation about faith / Veli-Matti Kärkkäinen.

Description: Eugene, OR: Cascade Books, 2026 | Includes bibliographical references.

Identifiers: ISBN 978-1-7252-7670-3 (paperback) | ISBN 978-1-7252-7671-0 (hardcover) | ISBN 978-1-7252-7672-7 (ebook)

Subjects: LCSH: Christianity and other religions—Islam. | Islam—Relations—Christianity. | Jesus Christ—Islamic interpretations.

Classification: BP172 K37 2026 (paperback) | BP172 K37 (ebook)

VERSION NUMBER 02/25/26

Hadith texts are from the Hadith Collection website: https://sunnah.com/.

Contents

Preface

THE BASIC IDEA BEHIND this book is simple and straightforward. I wish to present an accessible conversation between Muslims and Christians on topics of faith and theology that command mutual interest. In the Introduction below, I argue why this particular exchange of ideas between the currently two largest world religions is essential and useful to all Christians; even our Muslim friends may benefit from this conversation.

Having written a number of academic texts in the comparative mode, including the discussion between Christian and Muslim traditions, this one seeks to make accessible the more technical and at times cumbersome academic language. Anyone with interest in the topic, whether a layperson or a minister or a beginning student of theology, may read and engage it.

This text gleans from and in fact is based partially on my widely used 2019 academic textbook *Christian Theology in the Pluralistic World: A Global Introduction*[1] and its 2024 semi-academic version titled *I Believe. Help My Unbelief!: Christian Beliefs for a Religiously Pluralistic and Secular World.*[2] There are also borrowing and excerpts with little or no

1. That textbook of over 600 pages, with its careful bibliographic documentation, is based on a massive five-volume, highly technical theological project titled *A Constructive Christian Theology for the Pluralistic World*, published by Eerdmans (Grand Rapids) between 2013 and 2017: *Christ and Reconciliation* (2013), *Trinity and Revelation* (2014), *Creation and Humanity* (2015), *Spirit and Salvation* (2016), and *Community and Hope* (2017).

2. Kärkkäinen, *I Believe*.

change from my 2022 title *The End of All Things is at Hand: A Christian Eschatology in Conversation with Science and Islam.*[3]

While I wish to present a compelling account of Christian beliefs, I do not write this book as a hard-nosed apologist (a defender of faith) who wishes to convince the rest of the world of the rightness of Christian position. Rather, my approach is suggestive, inviting readers, whether Christians or Muslims, devoted or just interested in their own or another religion, into this conversation. That said, no one lays out a vision of a particular religion or another ideology without having confidence in its explanatory power, and even its salvific power (in the case of Christian faith). Hence, my approach is neither neutral nor uncommitted. At the same time, conviction and confidence do not have to translate into dogmatism or exclusivity.

I am greatly indebted to two wonderful institutions for allowing me to have the needed quiet place to write and a vibrant academic community to share parts of the contents of this book and receive most insightful feedback. The Polin Institute of Åbo Academy University in Turku, Finland provided me and my wife, Anne, a six-month long Research Fellowship in 2023–24. And the Collegeville Institute (formerly: The Institute for Ecumenical and Cultural Research) of St. John's University, Collegeville, Minnesota, provided us a semester-long Resident Scholar stay at the end of 2024. I can't possibly find words for the generosity and hospitality of these two innovative institutes. Furthermore, as always, my big thanks go to Fuller Theological Seminary in Pasadena, California for granting two Research Sabbaticals to make it possible to be freed from teaching and administrative duties. I can't think of any other academic institution more fully committed to providing her faculty members time and finances to research and write. As at the time of writing this manuscript I am about to complete my twenty-fifth year of professorial tenure at Fuller, let me dedicate this little book to this beloved community!

My thanks also go to Dr. Nick Scott-Blakely, a recent PhD from Fuller's Center for Advanced Theological Studies, for a most careful double-checking of all references and citations as well as compiling the bibliography.

3. Kärkkäinen, *End of All Things.* Because the current book borrows so widely from various parts of the said books of mine, it is not possible—nor helpful for the reader—to try to locate specific sections or ways it is dependent on them.

Introduction

Why and How to Compare Notes Between Christians and Muslims?

Why, in the First Place, to Carry a Conversation Between These Two Traditions?

If for no other reason than the fact that currently over 60 percent of the world's population are either Muslims or Christians—and, predictably, soon about three-fourths of the people on this earth—conversation and communication between the two Abrahamic faiths is an urgent task and opportunity. As it goes between these two giant religious camps, so it is with the world peace. The relationship between these two religious giants carries implications way beyond religion!

The global influence of these two world faiths is on the rise. Whereas Christianity is the largest religion with 2.4 billion adherents, Islam's current 1.7 billion number may outgrow Christians by 2050, making it the religion with the most adherents. What makes these two faith traditions' influences so massive in the contemporary world is that they are the only two religions with global presence, as opposed to say, Hinduism, which is a "local" religion of the subcontinent of India. Roughly equal numbers of Christians live in Europe, North America, Latin America, and the Caribbean, as well as sub-Saharan Africa. Muslims are also fairly evenly spread out, although a majority (over 60 percent) live in Pacific Asia, and the rest in Africa and the Middle East.

Compare that to the relatively small number of those without any definite religious commitment or confession. Globally speaking they represent a small minority, about 1.1 billion—even if secularism and the number of "nones" (people with no religious affiliation) is steadily growing in many parts of the world. Counterintuitively, to the surprise of the "prophets of secularism," what had been expected to become a religionless world with the progress of modernity and secular worldview has become even more religious.

Theology and the Christian church has until recently not minded the importance of other faiths in the way it should. In fact, one of the direst liabilities of Christian theology has been its oblivion to other faith traditions. Theology has been taught, studied, and written as if the world had only one religion, without due attention to the great diversity of religious teachings and beliefs. While other faiths also merit attention—just think of Hindus with about 1 billion or Buddhism with a half-billion adherents—the dialogue between Islam and Christianity, as mentioned, is even more urgent as its reverberations go beyond religious beliefs all the way to peace and well-being of the whole world.

How Does the Comparison Work—and Whether It Can Be Done Well?

Against the typical misconception, comparison between different religious traditions is a tedious and complex task. Whereas those not acquainted with the habits and obstacles in the comparative work readily pronounce judgments and opinions about the religious Other, even a casual acquaintance with the complexity of the task makes one modest and humble.

Just think of the complexity of any living faith tradition in itself, ours included, and you begin to fathom the challenges of comparison. There are many kinds of Christians in the world, similarly to, say, Muslims. There hardly is one normative, one-size-fits-all stereotype. Even when sharing some common normative beliefs, not all Muslims or Christian believe alike. Just consider the foundational sacred Scriptures as the basis of both of these Abrahamic traditions: among the Christian and Muslim readers and interpreters of the Bible and the Qur'an, there are a number of internal disputes, debates, and even mutual condemnations!

With that in mind, between Muslims and Christians we are attempting comparisons between two diverse worldwide communities in which

- one takes the Bible, the other the Qur'an as the highest authority
- one confesses faith in the Triune God whereas for the other it is the gravest sin in its denial of Allah's absolute unity
- one places all hopes of salvation for the atoning work of Jesus Christ on the cross and resurrection whereas for the other Jesus is only an important Prophet but has nothing to do with salvation of men and women—salvation comes only by way of submitting to Allah
- and so forth.

All of this raises the question of whether a useful and accurate comparison between Islam and Christian faith is even possible in the first place. Well-acquainted with all of these, and related, challenges, I still believe that a careful, respectful, and humble comparative work is possible and feasible. Yes, differences between the two traditions are significant and important. They should be acknowledged and even highlighted. Anyone attempting a comparison should not seek to whitewash, let alone ignore, foundational differences. Comparison is useful and interesting only to the point that the differences are being acknowledged. Why compare between two belief systems if both parties make every effort to "please" the other by denying one's own identity and deepest beliefs?

But what about the fact that in this case a Christian, that is a non-Muslim, seeks to explain and engage a faith other than his or her own? Is that justified or even helpful particularly in light of the fact that I am a Christian theologian, not an Islamicist (an academically trained specialist in the history, Scriptures, language, and other defining features of that religion)? This is a challenge to be reckoned with. What makes my task justified, I believe, is that I do not claim to be any kind of expert on Islam. Rather, my comments on that cousin faith are based on the scholarship and expertise of both Islamic and Christian scholars. Even when in this primer I use a minimum number of scholarly references, I hasten to mention that behind this semi-academic text is a huge scholarship from which I have learned. Furthermore, I approach the task from the stated Christian perspective. Ideally, a Muslim scholar would write a similar kind of book looking at the comparative task from his or her insider perspective. I am heartened and encouraged by a comment from Carole Hillenbrand, a noted Islamicist:

> I regard it as a serious misconception that only a Muslim could write a book like this [an introduction to Islam]. Indeed, I would argue that it is easier for a non-Muslim scholar of Islam than for a Muslim to identify which questions about Islam are regularly asked by non-Muslims—be they students or the general public, those of other faiths, or those who have no religious faith at all.[1]

I also resonate with the comment by the British theologian Keith Ward, one of the pioneers in this kind of comparative work: "There is a tradition at the very heart of [many living] . . . faiths which is held [in] common. It is not that precisely the same doctrines are believed, but that the same tendencies of thought and devotion exist, and are expressed within rather diverse patterns of thought, characteristic of the faiths in question." At the same time, he notes that "religions generate infinite differences."[2] Therefore, we should be careful and modest in our work.

As said, comparative theology—as it is called technically—does not seek to brush aside or undermine deep differences around the dialogue table. This is because, properly done, comparative theology does not attempt to reach an agreement at any cost. An authentic work of comparison is never an exercise in compromise. Its end result may well be the clarification of differences in even more definite way rather than the discovery of some convergence. Talking to another tradition and getting to know it in a deeper way is in itself a valuable goal. It also gives an opportunity to clarify one's own beliefs. A constructive comparative work functions similarly to a mirror: it helps us discover more authentically what we ourselves "look like."

With these caveats in mind, it is useful to list the many benefits of careful, respectful comparative work.

> First, Christians can and should learn something about non-Christian religious traditions for the sake of the religious other; in fact, both the license and the imperative to do so rest on a biblical foundation. Second, Christians can and should expect to learn something about God in the course of that exploration, and the basis for such a belief can be found in who God has revealed Godself to be and how Christians have traditionally understood that divine self-revelation. Third, Christians can and should expect that their understanding of their own faith tradition will

1. Hillenbrand, *Introduction to Islam*, 20.
2. Ward, *Images of Eternity*, 1.

> be stretched and challenged, but at the same time deepened and strengthened through such interreligious dialogue.[3]

The Plan and Nature of the Book

Written by a Christian theologian, unabashedly from a Christian perspective, the topics and rubrics below follow that faith tradition. Commensurately, were there a Muslim writer, his or her outline would be drafted according to the belief system of Islam.

Before getting into the comparative work, chapter 1 is meant to provide a brief orientation to the basic history of the emergence of Islam and the Prophet's role therein. This makes it easier for a non-Muslim to follow the book's discussion even with little or no previous knowledge of that religious tradition.

Let me also mention as a way of orientation that because the teachings of the Qur'an are so foundational to Islam, including in the contemporary world, I base all of the main doctrines on the teachings of this primary Holy Scripture. Assuming that most Christians, even those with some interest in Islam, might not have ever read the Qur'an or have only a superficial knowledge about it, when referencing Muslims' Holy Book, I also include the direct citation either in the main text or in a footnote.

Following the basic introductory chapter to Islam, in light of the fact that both Christian and Muslim religions are "Religions of the Book," it is only fair to begin the actual comparative conversation with the focus on Scripture and revelation (chapter 2). Basically all claims by these two traditions boil down to their authoritative Scriptures and their trusted interpretations and commentaries. Particularly in Islam, the Holy Scripture plays a foundational and highly authoritative role in defining beliefs and doctrines.

Following revelation and Scripture, the most likely candidate for the comparison is of course the doctrine of God. This is a complex and delicate issue. On the one hand, similarly to both traditions' mother faith, Judaism, there is the challenge and promise of "proximity," that is, the fact that all Abrahamic faiths are strictly monotheistic. On the other hand, the Christian tradition's uncompromising monotheism in the form of a Trinitarian confession places a huge demand on Islam. Hence, chapter 3

3. Largen, *Baby Krishna*, 9.

seeks to address the question of the heading, namely whether Allah and Yahweh/the Father of Jesus Christ is the one and same God or not.

Following these two fundamental doctrines—namely, Scripture and God—more than one type of outline could be followed. Here is the way this book is structured. Chapter 4 delves into another highly significant topic for both traditions, namely the meaning and role of Jesus of Nazareth. As is well-known, Jesus plays a remarkable role in Islamic tradition—albeit differently from the Christian belief system. This topic is followed by the discussions of God's creation of the world and the human being as God's image as interpreted in these two traditions (chapters 5 and 6).

Even if salvation in Islam does not come from Jesus—nor, of course, from Muhammad—for a *Christian*-Muslim engagement an all-important theme relates to the twofold question of salvation: negatively, why do we need salvation or, to be more precise, what is wrong with us (chapter 7), a question about which these two Abrahamic traditions disagree sharply. The positive angle to the question of salvation is the Christian claim of Jesus as the bringer of salvation, a suggestion harshly rejected by Islam (chapter 8).

Although not a central doctrine in Muslim faith, the question of the Spirit of God merits a short deliberation (chapter 9). The final two chapters are standard in Christian presentation of beliefs, namely the role of the religious community—church in Christian and *ummah* in Muslim parlance—and its religious acts, named worship and sacraments by the Christians (chapter 10) and, finally, the "end" of all things, a.k.a. eschatology.

To repeat: This is a comparison attempted from a Christian perspective, by a Christian author, willing to learn more about Islam in a spirit of hospitality and mutual enrichment.

1

How Did Islam Emerge as a Major World Religion?

Assuming that most non-Muslim readers of this book may not be well—or even, at all—acquainted with that faith tradition, I dare to outline very briefly some of Islam's crucial historical and doctrinal aspects. You may recall that in the Introduction I justified this kind of modest attempt by an outsider to offer a brief sympathetic orientation to a religion other than one's own. At the same time, I am painfully aware of this brief primer's limitations and beg the reader's patience and understanding.

Let us begin from where Islam began, namely from the Prophet Muhammad's life-story. Even if the Prophet plays no divine role in Islam in a way Jesus Christ does in Christianity, his founding role of the new religion is critical and highly venerated.

The Prophet's Life-Story

Despite many gaps in our knowledge about the Prophet Muhammad's life-story,[1] it is far easier to study the origins and emergence of Islam than that of many other religions. The main reason is that—similarly to Buddhism and its founder Gautama Buddha—there is one single founder unlike, say, in Judaism and Hinduism.

1. Throughout this section and beyond I have consulted for details and accuracy of facts the standard work by F. E. Peters, *Muhammad and the Origins of Islam*.

Muhammad was born around 570 AD into a wealthy Quraysh tribe in Mecca, a clan which had gathered its fortunes by caravan trade. That said, tradition has it that he was orphaned young (see Qur'an [hereafter Q] 93:6–10[2]) and raised by his uncle Abu Talib, whose son, Muhammad's cousin, became his early and most important follower. Hired by a wealthy widow, Khadija, to work for the safety of caravans, Muhammad later married her at the age of around twenty-five years. The work of merchant became his main occupation.

The area in which the Prophet grew was fertile for religions and cults. Many gods and goddesses were venerated and worshipped. "Bedouin cultic practices were animistic, involving the worship of idols, stones, and trees, and the Bedouin would run or walk round (circumambulate) these sacred objects a prescribed number of times. Soothsayers (*kahins*) performed a variety of shamanistic roles."[3]

Nearing the age of forty, in Mecca Muhammad began to withdraw to places of solitude to meditate and search for truth and peace. In a cave called Hira on the Mountain of Light he received his first revelation. What is widely considered to be the very first saying in the Qur'an was allegedly revealed to him at this time: "Recite: In the Name of your Lord Who created . . ." (Q 96:1).

Beginning from this angelic visitation, divine revelations became the basis of what is now known as the Qur'an. Its main message was a stark condemnation of the widespread polytheism (belief in many gods) in the Arabian Peninsula. Hence, the doctrine of absolute oneness of God became the focus of the new emerging religion. After a few years following the revelations, Muhammad began to preach the message beyond his own family.

Whereas the uncompromising monotheism (belief in one God) raised opposition among the many merchants who feared that it might stifle their trade, the new religion began to gain support both in his own family and soon also among others. That said, the majority of his own clan turned against him. Eventually, the opposition grew strong enough for Muhammad and his extended family to have to move to Medina around 622. Known as *hijra*, this flight marks year 1 on the Muslim calendar.

2. "Did He not find you an orphan and shelter you? And did He not find you erring and guided you? And did He not find you needy and enrich you? So, as for the orphan, do not oppress [him], and as for the beggar, do not drive [him] away . . ." (Q 93:6–10).

3. Hillenbrand, *Introduction to Islam*, 25.

The divine messages and visitations continued, including the famous Night Journey into the heaven (referred to also in Q 17:1[4]):

> One night, while the Prophet was sleeping, the Archangel Gabriel came and led him on a journey. Mounted on the heavenly steed Buraq, Muhammad traveled from the Ka'ba in Mecca to the "Farthest Mosque," which Muslims believe to be the Al-Aqsa Mosque in Jerusalem. There he prayed with other prophets such as Moses, Abraham, and Jesus, and ascended to the skies, where he was led by Gabriel through Paradise and Hell, and finally came face to face with God. He then returned to earth to continue spreading the message of Islam. According to Islamic belief, Muhammad was the only person to see Heaven and Hell while still alive.[5]

After tumultuous events, Muhammad was able to return to Mecca and both with persuasion and force to take over the city and make it the prime center of Islam. During that period the divine revelations were completed as the basis for the Qur'an. Hence, we speak of Meccan and Medinan suras (chapters of the Qur'an) about which more below in chapter 2.

After the death of his first wife, who bore a number of sons (all of whom probably died in infancy) and four daughters to him, Muhammad married again a number of times (tradition has it that he did so at least ten times). His favorite and most beloved wife was Aisha, whom he chose at her pre-puberty. Her father was Abu Bakr, one of the first "founding" khalifs (early leaders) after the Prophet's death. Muhammad's favorite daughter Fatima married Ali, his cousin.

Most likely Muhammad had some dealings with both Jews and Christians, as their presence in the Mecca and surrounding areas had become stronger by the end of the sixth century. As is often claimed, probably with due justification, he had more contacts with heretical Christians than orthodox ones—"heretical" meaning those whose Christology and the doctrine of the Trinity deviated from the consensus of the early Christian creeds. That said, it is a difficult task to try to sort out how much of Muhammad's take on Christianity is a function of these heretical Christian teachings.

4. "Glory be to Him Who carried His servant by night from the Sacred Mosque to the Farthest Mosque; the environs of which We have blessed, that We might show him some of Our signs. Indeed He is the Hearing, the Seeing" (Q 17:1).

5. Metropolitan Museum of Art, "Prophet Muhammad."

The Emergence and Split of the Islamic Community

As is well-known, the emerging Muslim community, *ummah*, was split in Islam's early history. The same division has continued since between the Sunni and the Shi'ites. This major division arose mainly over the issue of the Prophet's successor after his death (632).

The father of the Prophet's beloved wife Aisha, Abu Bakr, was made the first leader by the majority, but that did not settle the matter. The minority of the community preferred as their leader Ali, the husband of Muhammad's daughter Fatima. Both theological and political issues were involved.

Whereas for the majority the leadership choice after the passing of the Prophet belonged to the *ummah* at large, for the rest it was God's choice falling on Ali—with the ambiguous claim that he had both the divine and the Prophet's endorsement. While the majority (the origin of the Sunnis) wanted to stay in the line of Mecca's dominant tribe, the Prophet's own tribe, Quraysh, a minority (the origin of the Shi'ites) received support from Medina. This led to the final separation by the mid-sixth century. Currently over 80 percent of the global Islam belongs to the Sunnis and the rest to the Shi'ites, each side having a large number of denominations.

What is remarkable about this split—to be discussed in more detail in chapter 10—is that both of these main groupings endorse all major Muslim doctrines based on the divine revelation in the Qur'an and focused on God's unity and Muhammad's mediatory role of revelation. Even in spiritual practices there are only minor differences!

With these humble origins, Islam is currently among the two biggest world religions. Its number approaches and is likely to hit 2 billion before the end of the 2020s. The growth is attributed primarily to birth rate.

The main centers of global Islam include South Asia, which houses about one-third of Muslims, Indonesia being the biggest single Muslim country in the world. India has more Muslims than any other non-Muslim country, about 200 million. In the Middle East and North Africa about a quarter of Muslims reside. Sub-Saharan Africa similarly has a large Muslim population and noteworthy are pockets of Muslims in Russia, China, Europe, and North America.

Legendary Traditions About the Prophet

Moving beyond more or less academically ratified common knowledge about Islam and its founder, we hasten to remind the non-Muslim reader that there is a deep and wide tradition of miraculous, supernatural events associated with the Prophet. These form a common belief system among virtually all Muslim denominations and sects.

Recorded in the *Sira[h]*, legendary biographies of the Prophet, there is a prophecy about the birth of the Prophet somewhat similar to the birth of some Jewish prophets and Jesus Christ, as well as, say, Gautama Buddha. Why is this important?

Such ratifying of the prophethood of Muhammad is very important to the credibility of the revelation he brought to humankind. Moreover, just as the coming and the birth of Jesus are heralded by heavenly portents such as the star of Bethlehem, the Annunciation to Mary, and the virgin birth, so too with Muhammad. His birth is announced to his mother, Amina, by a voice that has sometimes been thought to be Gabriel's. When Muhammad is born, Amina says that she saw a light coming out from her that illuminated the space between east and west. An even more famous miraculous episode is recorded in the sira when in his early childhood Muhammad's breast is opened up by two angels who cleanse his heart.[6]

That said, it is essential for the non-Muslim reader to know that in Muslim teaching the Prophet is but a human being, neither divine, nor a savior as is the case with Jesus Christ for Christians. Just think of the oft-cited Qur'anic statement: "Say: 'I am only a human being like you . . .'" (Q 18:110). Nor is there any claim for Muhammad's sinlessness, although his piety and devotion to Allah is praised and emulated.

Even if the Muslim tradition does not appreciate the "Suffering Servant" type of spirituality after Jewish and Christian traditions in its depiction of Muhammad as a victorious champion, nor does the *Sunna[h]*, the vast tradition of the Prophet's sayings and life events, hide some of his misdeeds and failures as a human being. In fact, the standard Muslim tradition has it that Muhammad was illiterate, "the unlettered prophet" (Q 7:157). "And thou wast not (able) to recite a Book before this (Book came), nor art thou (able) to transcribe it with thy right hand . . ." (Q 29:48, Abdullah Yusuf Ali trans.). That said, neither is there any written

6. Hillenbrand, *Introduction to Islam*, 43.

record authored by Jesus of Nazareth. And keep in mind that the vast majority of people at the time were not literate.

At the same time, it is also to be noted that—similarly to most living faith traditions—in folk Islam, particularly in various Sufi movements and communities penetrated with deep spiritual devotion of Sufism—the Prophet's role and status is highly elevated and venerated. In fact, it is elevated to a level which tests, and at times, transgresses orthodox Islam's strict insistence on the uniqueness of Allah without any violation of *shirk*, the gravest sin of associating the Deity with anything created.

An important Muslim way of honoring the Prophet is the great celebration of his birth date (as much debated as the exact date might be among the critical scholars). This feast is particularly significant among most Shi'a movements, although not limited to them. Another common way of respecting the Prophet is the rich poetry tradition in various languages, some of them going back to early history. One grand example is the well-known "The Poem of the Cloak," written in the thirteenth century by Imam al-Busiri. He wrote the poem to thank the Prophet for wrapping him in a cloak in a dream, signifying forgiveness and divine favor.[7] Not for nothing, many commentaries have been written on this beloved piece of art.

A key guide to all Muslims, particularly for leaders, is the extensive, above-mentioned *Sunnah*, the tradition and legacy of the Muhammad's deeds and actions. It consists of vast *Hadith* literature and comes in three interrelated forms: the Prophet's sayings, deeds, and practices.[8]

God's Unity and the Holy Qur'an as the Foundation of Islam

Before getting into many individual beliefs and doctrines between the two cousin traditions, it is helpful to attempt a bird's-eye view of Islam's key theological position and vision. This hopefully helps you to see the forest from the trees.

This bigger picture is important also in the sense that both in Islam and Christianity, it is not only about certain beliefs and doctrines, as much as it is also that; behind both traditions stands a bigger vision of the world—and God's place therein. In other words, there is the idea of a

7. In Arabic the poem is called *Qasida al-Burda*. See Al-Busiri, *Mantle Adorned*.

8. At times Hadith is reserved only for the Prophet's sayings and the Sunnah for his actions and practices. The terminology is somewhat vacillating.

Christian—or a Muslim—interpretation of all that there is, including but not limited to human life. If God is the creator of everything, as Christian do believe, then as the medieval Christian genius Thomas Aquinas would claim, the object of theology is God *and* everything in relation to God, precisely because God has created everything. The same principle applies to Islam.

Based on this God-centered vision of faith and the world, the two defining and most critical tenets of faith for Islam are God's unity and the divine revelation in the Qur'an, to be discussed in more detail below. These two cannot be compromised, nor changed. They define the basic core of Islam's faith and religion. Are there any creeds in Islam, short statements crystallizing the core beliefs and vision? Yes, there are a few, although they seem not to play as central role as they do in Christianity, particularly among the liturgical churches' regular worship cycle.

Now, after this all-too brief orientation to Islam's history and vision, we are ready to embark on our journey through key beliefs and their Christian counterparts.

2

Are Both the Bible and Qur'an Divine Revelation?

As with most chapters, our first task in this chapter is to summarize very briefly key aspects of the Christian understanding of the Bible and divine revelation. This is necessary for a meaningful comparison with the Islamic theology of revelation. Thereafter, Islam's high view of Scripture and divine revelation will be explained. Following, we will consider the ways Holy Scripture functions between these two faith traditions, both of which claim the Jewish Torah (Christian Old Testament) as the founding divine revelation. This makes it possible to consider some of the differences between the Christian view of the Bible and the Muslim view of the Qur'an, an equally important task for any authentic comparison.

This is What (Most) Christians Believe About the Bible and Scripture

In Christian understanding, God's revelation comes in many forms, not only in the Bible although the written Scripture is the authoritative access to the divine revelation. Most foundationally divine revelation comes in the person and work of Jesus Christ, the Word made flesh, the incarnated Son of God. Jesus' coming is preceded by the long history of God's dealings with the people of Israel and other nations, the narrative of the Old Testament. Christian tradition also believes that some kind of preparatory and useful revelation—named general revelation—can be found in the world created by God, history guided by the same God, and in humanity, having been created in God's image.

Although the Bible contains divine revelation, as a written book it is also fully human product. Rightly understood, it can be said that the written Word testifies to and gives us access to the living Word, Christ (John 1:1), who became one of us in incarnation, God-with-Us (1:14).

The Bible is a book written by more than forty authors, many of whom remain unknown to us. They wrote over a very long period of time, stretching over a millennium. The authors, both the ones who are known by name (and in many cases, with some personal history) and those unknown, come from many walks of life, from different cultures, and from diverse personal and communal experiences. No wonder, then, that the Bible comes to us in many literary forms, from poetry and proverbs, to teaching and sermons, to personal and communal narratives and nations' histories, and so forth.

The divine revelation in the Bible is thus deeply involved in history, both world history and history of the communities and nations, particularly the people of God, Israel, and the new people of God in the New Testament, the church. Christian theology has always believed that there is a progression in God's revelation of his will in that the further the biblical history progresses, the deeper the grasping of divine revelation is developing. The summit of revelation is Jesus Christ. Briefly put: while divine in origin, Christian revelation is historical, embedded in history, and also progressive, as it unfolds slowly amidst the people of God.

To use theological language, revelation is a Trinitarian process: out of his abundant love the Father reaches out to humanity in order to establish a fellowship, by sending his Son to be one of us, to die and be raised to new life, in the power of the Spirit. This same Spirit is also believed to have inspired the Scripture and to continuously make it lively.

While all Christian churches consider the Bible, whose first part (in Christian parlance), the Old Testament, is shared with the Jewish mother faith, as authoritative and as a special channel of revelation, modern Christianity also endorses the importance of historical and critical study of its message. Whereas up until the time of the Enlightenment in the eighteenth century, the Bible was universally believed to be more or less inerrant (at least in substance), in modernity, alongside the rise of historical-critical study, the now famous division between "conservative" (fundamentalist) and "liberal" approaches emerged. Whereas the former makes every effort to stick closer to the premodern attitude, the latter embraces more enthusiastically the results and insights of the critical study. Between these two extremes lie all kinds of variations. That said: a proper historical-critical study is endorsed by most.

Notwithstanding all the disputes concerning the nature of Scripture as revelation and the nature of its inspiration, all Christians agree that in some real sense the Bible is God's word in human words. In other words, it has neither come directly from God, as in dictation, nor is it merely humans talking to each other about human experiences of the sacred.

The great dispute at the time of the Protestant Reformation in the sixteenth century related to the relationship between revelation in written Scripture and its continuing growth in church tradition. It took hundreds of years for the churches on both sides of the divide to come to understand that this is not an either-or matter but rather a both-and. While it is currently a consensus that the Scripture is the highest norm of faith and practice, it is also acknowledged that the formation and final ratification of the Bible as Scripture by the church community are not alternatives but rather mutually conditioning each other.

The Holy Qur'an as the Living, Authoritative Revelation of Allah[1]

Perhaps no other living religion honors her Sacred Scripture as highly as does Islam. Somewhat similarly to how Hindus view the Vedas, most Muslims consider the Qur'an the eternal speech of God.[2] It lays the foundation for the religion, community, and way of life. "Out of the Qur'an arises the Islamic community, its law, literature, art, and religion. Perhaps more than any other religious community, Muslims are a 'people of the Book.'"[3] The Holy Qur'an is the beginning and the end of all Muslim thinking and living religiously.

Although the Prophet Muhammad, as mentioned, is not a divine figure in Islam, nor a "savior," his role as the recipient of the Qur'anic

1. Alongside my earlier publications, as detailed in the Preface above, my exposition is indebted throughout this chapter to Hillenbrand, *Introduction to Islam*, 58–88.

2. This official point notwithstanding, there is the minority opinion according to which Qur'an was created in time or history. That said, all Muslims assign high, divine status to Scripture.

3. Coward, *Sacred Word*, 81.

revelation is unsurpassable: "God is the speaker of the revelation, the angel Gabriel is the intermediary agent, and Muhammad is the recipient."[4]

Although the reception by the Prophet did not happen in one event but rather was a succession of divine visitations, most memorable is what is now known as the last of the ten nights of Ramadan, a pivotal moment in Islam's annual cycle:

> It was in the year 610 during one of the last ten nights of Ramadan, known as the Night of Power . . . that, according to Islamic belief, the Qur'an descended in full into the soul of Muhammad: "We sent it down on the Night of Power. What will explain to you what that Night of Power is? The Night of Power is better than a thousand months" (97:1).[5]

No wonder, then, that during the month of Ramadan, the faithful Muslim is supposed to recite the whole Qur'an.

According to the tradition, the angel Gabriel conveyed the whole Qur'an during the period of about a quarter-century.[6] And once the revelation was complete, the angel recited it twice to the Prophet. Hence, Islam regards the Qur'an as the direct, authoritative speech of God conveyed through the Prophet. In fact, it is believed that the human person unaided would not be able to produce even one *sura* of it.[7]

Importantly, it is believed that his divine revelation was received in its authentic and pure form only in its original Arabic, which is a holy language as taught in the Qur'an itself: "And thus have We revealed to you an Arabic Qur'ān" (Q 42:7). Indeed, there is an old tradition according to which the Qur'an is but a copy of a "Guarded Tablet" in heaven (Q 85:21–22).[8] No wonder that Muslims believe in the strict infallibility of the Qur'an in its original language. That said, similarly to other Abrahamic traditions, no original manuscript has survived to this day of what

4. Coward, *Sacred Word*, 82.

5. Hillenbrand, *Introduction to Islam*, 102 (the Qur'anic translation used in the book is followed here).

6. "And [it is] a Qur'ān that We have divided that you may recite it to mankind at intervals, and We have revealed it by [successive] revelation" (Q 17:106).

7. "And if you are in doubt concerning what We have revealed to Our servant, then bring a sūra like it; and call your witnesses besides God if you are truthful. And if you do not and you will not, then fear the Fire, whose fuel is men, and stones, prepared for disbelievers" (Q 2:23–24).

8. "Nay, but it is a glorious Qur'ān, in a tablet, preserved" (Q 85:21–22).

is believed to be the first canonized inscription some time after Muhammad's day! The Prophet's companions produced the written edition.

This means that any translation from the Arabic is but a *translation* rather than strictly speaking the essential Word of God. At the same time, the Qur'an in languages other than Arabic is useful and even necessary for non-Arabic speakers, even if of lower revelatory status. Not only that: the most authentic way for human beings to experience the fullness of Qur'anic revelation is to hear it recited in Arabic. Here, there is similarity to Hinduism, in which the spoken word is primary, the written secondary. That said, Islam also assigns due importance to reading Scripture in Arabic as well. Namely, the term *Qur'an* in Arabic means both "recitation" and "reading," thus embracing both oral and written aspects.

A useful way to divide the Qur'an in two major parts has to do with the distinction between the so-called Meccan and Medinan [or: Madinan] suras. While no complete scholarly consensus can be found, the outline of this distinction is fairly clear:

> The Meccan surahs are the surahs that were revealed to the Prophet (peace and blessings of Allah be upon him) during his residence in Mecca. While Medinan surahs were revealed to the Prophet (peace and blessings be upon him) after his migration to Madinah. Meccan surahs mainly focus on and discuss matters such as Tawheed (monotheism), the day of judgment and the afterlife, the punishment of the disbelievers, and Prophethood. Additionally, they are shorter than the Madani surahs. On the other hand, Medinan Suras are longer and deal with topics regarding faith, Islamic rulings, and worshipping Allah. They were revealed to teach Muslims how to live their lives. In short, Meccan and Madani surahs differ in the subject matter, length, and style.[9]

Like the New Testament, the Qur'an defines its main and ultimate goal as the salvation of humankind (although "salvation" in Islam is different from the Christian view, as we will explain below). The Holy Qur'an often refers to itself as the guide or path to salvation and true knowledge of God: "A Book We have revealed to you that you may bring forth mankind from darkness into light by the leave of their Lord to the path of the Mighty, the Praised" (Q 14:1). Islam holds a firm belief that great blessings come from this recital, not only in this life but also in the

9. Studio Arabiya Institute, "Difference Between," paras. 13–16.

life to come. "The Qur'an is uttered to call others to it, to expiate sins, to protect against punishment, and to ensure blessings in paradise."[10]

No wonder, then, that a very high view of the infallibility of the Qur'anic revelation and words is affirmed by all orthodox Muslim traditions. Sura 11, which speaks of Muhammad's task as prophet, opens with this affirmation: "(This is) a Scripture the revelations whereof are perfected and then expounded. (It cometh) from One Wise, Informed" (Q 11:1, Marmaduke Pickthall trans.). According to Q 2:2, "That Book, in it there is no doubt . . ."

Not surprisingly, the Islamic tradition has paid close attention to careful and authoritative exegesis (*tafsir*) of the Qur'an. Because the Qur'an lays the foundation for and regulates all aspects of life and society, more is at stake in the hermeneutics of Scripture in Islam than with most other traditions. Conversely, Christians and other non-Muslims are accused of false interpretation, or indeed of "alteration" (*tahrif*). A major asset of polemics against Christians and others is to dispute their way of interpreting Scripture.

Holy Scripture Between the Two Faith Traditions

Muslims, alongside Jews and Christians, are called the "People of the Book." Why so? Because of the necessary and authoritative role played by the written canonical Scripture. Not so with all religions: for example, in Hinduism, the spoken word is primary, the written secondary. In fact, it is interesting that in one sense Islam combines both worlds, namely the oral and written when it comes to the revealed book.

The importance of the Scripture in the Muslim-Christian encounter is heightened by the fact that the Qur'an does not do away with earlier revelations, Israel's Torah and the Christian Bible. Rather, it considers itself their fulfillment and correction. Well-known is the statement in Qur'an 42:15 that clearly bespeaks universality: "I believe in whatever Book God has revealed." Or this one from Q 3:64: "Say: 'O People of the Scripture! Come now to a word agreed upon between us and you, that we worship none but God.'" This means that in Islamic understanding there is a robust continuity between it and the other two Abrahamic faiths, particularly Judaism. Not only that but one part of the Qur'anic teaching seems to assume that the divine revelation as guide is available to all

10. Coward, *Sacred Word*, 85–86.

nations: "Verily We have sent thee in truth, as a bearer of glad tidings, and as a warner: and there never was a people, without a warner having lived among them (in the past)" (Q 35:24, Abdullah Yusuf Ali trans.).

That said, Islam believes that it helps correct, fine-tune, and bring to fulfillment the divine revelation that began with the people of Israel. It considers itself as the fulfillment of God's revelation. As a result, there is a determined insistence on the supremacy and finality of the Qur'anic revelation. Q 5:44–48[11] makes this clear by presenting the Jewish Torah and the Christian New Testament as stepping-stones to the final revelation given in the Qur'an. Not only does the Qur'an provide fulfillment; it also provides correction and criteria. It is in light of the Qur'an that the value of other revelations is assessed.

Islam and Christianity share the commonality of having a closed canon, whereas in Buddhism and Hinduism the borders of the canon are much more fluid and elusive. That said, similarly to other main faith traditions, linked to later exposition and expansion of the primary Qur'anic materials, a huge and vast secondary Hadith tradition also exists, which consists of the sayings of the Prophet and other sages. The sayings and actions of Muhammad narrated in the Hadith are believed not to be revealed, although they are inspired.

11. "It was We who revealed the law (to Moses): therein was guidance and light. By its standard have been judged the Jews, by the prophets who bowed (as in Islam) to Allah's will, by the rabbis and the doctors of law: for to them was entrusted the protection of Allah's book, and they were witnesses thereto: therefore fear not men, but fear me, and sell not my signs for a miserable price. If any do fail to judge by (the light of) what Allah hath revealed, they are (no better than) Unbelievers. We ordained therein for them: 'Life for life, eye for eye, nose or nose, ear for ear, tooth for tooth, and wounds equal for equal.' But if any one remits the retaliation by way of charity, it is an act of atonement for himself. And if any fail to judge by (the light of) what Allah hath revealed, they are (no better than) wrong-doers. And in their footsteps We sent Jesus the son of Mary, confirming the Law that had come before him: We sent him the Gospel: therein was guidance and light, and confirmation of the Law that had come before him: a guidance and an admonition to those who fear Allah. Let the people of the Gospel judge by what Allah hath revealed therein. If any do fail to judge by (the light of) what Allah hath revealed, they are (no better than) those who rebel. To thee We sent the Scripture in truth, confirming the scripture that came before it, and guarding it in safety: so judge between them by what Allah hath revealed, and follow not their vain desires, diverging from the Truth that hath come to thee. To each among you have we prescribed a law and an open way. If Allah had so willed, He would have made you a single people, but (His plan is) to test you in what He hath given you: so strive as in a race in all virtues. The goal of you all is to Allah. It is He that will show you the truth of the matters in which ye dispute" (Q 5:44–48, Abdullah Yusuf Ali trans.).

Originally, the number of the Hadith is immense, later condensed into about 25,000. By far the most important is the Hadith of Bukkhari; significant is also the Hadith of Muslim, among others. The Christian counterpart to the post-biblical sacred literature is the vast collection of the writings of church fathers and later teachers and theologians of the church.

Both traditions have also brought about a huge number of commentary literature, similar to that of other living faiths. Particularly the mainline Sunni exegesis during the first Islamic centuries became very famous for its meticulous and tedious work. Along with the mainline Sunni and Shi'ite schools, the mystical Sufi schools have produced an amazingly diverse devotional and mystical literary and poetic treasury.

While in Islam the Qur'an serves as the guide to the right path and therefore its didactic value is highly sought, there is also a deep devotional element similar to other Abrahamic traditions. The following verse could easily be found in Jewish or Christian Scriptures: "And when they hear what has been revealed to the Messenger, you see their eyes overflow with tears because of what they recognise of the truth. They say, 'Our Lord, we believe, so inscribe us among the witnesses'" (Q 5:83).

The Ways the Qur'an and the Bible Differ from Each Other

Compared to Christian and Jewish Scriptures—let alone the major Asiatic faiths—Islam's Holy Book is very short, only 114 suras (chapters),[12] shorter than the New Testament. A major difference also has to do with it nature: there is no plot, no narrative. It is composed of sayings. Its structure follows quite closely the length of the sura, in descending order. Hence, the opening suras are by far the longest (with a few long ones in other parts).

Islam's claim for the uniqueness of its Arabic language, a highly treasured feature in that religion, is strange to Jewish-Christian tradition. Interestingly, the form of Arabic used in the Qur'an is of the tribe of Quraysh, that of Muhammad. Stylistically it is identical with none of the known bodies of Arabic. Even the Arabic of the Hadiths is different from that of the Qur'an.

Other distinguishing features include that there is basically only one author when compared to Jewish and Christian Scriptures. On the

12. Suras are known by names that were added later. Fortunately, non-Muslims may use numbering as an aid to find certain passages.

contrary, in the Bible, composed over a long period of time, tens and tens of authors served as contributors, many of whose names and even life stories are unknown to us. Christians believe that the divine revelation was given to men and women in various forms including divine speech, parables, teachings, proverbs, and poetry. And it came through various circumstances ranging from divine encounters and struggles with God, to dreams and visions, and so forth. Hence, in Christian understanding the Word of God is fully divine and fully human. This is a dramatic difference as in the Qur'an "there is no notion of an inspiration from God that is then clothed and uttered in the best words a human mind can create. In the Qur'an, Muhammad receives a direct, fully composed revelation from God, which he then recites to others."[13]

Whereas both Jewish (and particularly earlier) Christian traditions encourage memorization of Scripture, Islam emphasizes it in a very special manner. "A person who has memorized the whole of the Qur'an . . . is much respected, and their number may well run into the hundreds of thousands." And consider this: "Teaching the Qur'an in prison in Saudi Arabia is an old tradition; after the passing of two decrees (1987 and 1990), prisoners who have learned the entire Qur'an, or parts of it, by heart can receive a remission in their sentences."[14]

Whereas in all Abrahamic traditions the Holy Scripture serves as a major guide to devotion and is looked for as a guide to true faith and life, the Qur'an because of its extremely high divine nature is considered to have almost magical power and force:

> Had We sent down this Qur'an on a mountain, verily, thou wouldst have seen it humble itself and cleave asunder for fear of God. Such are the similitudes which We propound to men, that they may reflect (Q 59:21).

In the same vein, consider this dramatic description:

> In addition to its destructive power, the words of the Qur'an are also a positive source for healing and tranquility. According to tradition when the Qur'an is recited divine tranquility (*sakīnah*) descends, mercy covers the reciters, angels draw near to them, and God remembers them. Tradition also tells how one of the companions of Muhammad came to him and reported seeing something like lamps between heaven and earth as he

13. Coward, *Sacred Word*, 82.

14. Hillenbrand, *Introduction to Islam*, 78.

> recited while riding horseback during the night. Muhammad is reported to have said that the lights were angels descended to hear the recitation of the Qur'an. For the pious Muslim, then, the chanted words of the Qur'an have the numinous power to cause destruction, to bring mercy, to provide protection, to give knowledge, and to evoke miraculous signs.[15]

As mentioned, the nature and structure of the Qur'an and the Bible differs dramatically from each other. Whereas the Bible at large consists of a big narrative, from creation in the beginning to the final consummation in the end, in the Qur'an there is nothing like that. It is rather a collection of scattered, largely unrelated sayings, exhortations, and occasional stories (often without a sustained narrative plot). This is markedly different from large portions of the Bible, both the Old Testament and New Testament, in which narratives such as those related to the people of Israel or to the life of Jesus or to the history of the early church dominate. The Bible is also significantly bigger with sixty-six books; even the New Testament is much larger than the Qur'an, four-fifths bigger. Because of its very nature, without a narrative plot, consisting of numerous sayings and similar, the Qur'an makes challenging reading. It is not easy to understand.

Unlike in contemporary Christian theology, in which the tools of critical scholarship even among those who uphold the classical divine inspiration of Scripture is common, Orthodox Islam does not allow any such critical scrutiny (apart from academicians working outside Muslim heartlands in the secular Western academia). Where critical contemporary scholars, mainly based in the West, acknowledge the personal, religious, sociohistorical, and similar contextual factors in the formation of the canon, orthodox Islam regards the Arabic Qur'an as the direct, authoritative speech of God conveyed through the Prophet. Unlike the Christian understanding of the formation of the canon as a centuries-long, divine-human synergy, orthodox Islam rests on the firm conviction that the formation and closing of the Qur'anic canon were a divine act through Muhammad without any human mediation.

All that said, we have to acknowledge the deep, continuing debates within Christian tradition about the nature of divine revelation and biblical criticism. The British comparative theologian Clinton Bennett

15. Coward, *Sacred Word*, 86.

succinctly lays out this complexity—which, of course, is an urgent invitation to continuing careful dialogue:

> In many respects, the conservative Christian view of the Bible as infallible and as inspired word for word is closer to how Muslims view the Qur'an than to the liberal Christian view of the Bible as a potentially fallible, human response to experience of the divine. On the Muslim right, the Bible is regarded as so corrupt that it no longer has any value. On the Christian left, an attempt is made to understand how the Qur'an can be accepted as "revelation." One difficulty is that Christians who deconstruct the Bible are likely to transfer this approach to the Qur'an as well, which is unacceptable, even to more liberal Muslims. Yet despite each side's view of the Other's scripture, Christians and Muslims from both the "right" and "left" cite from the Other's scripture to support their views. Christians have their favourite Qur'anic passages while Muslims have favourite Bible passages. More often than not, when Christians and Muslims use each other's scriptures, they do so in a manner that ignores or refutes how Christians and Muslims understand the passages concerned.[16]

16. Bennett, *Understanding Christian-Muslim Relations*, 16.

3

Triune God and Allah

Same God or Different Gods?

The Distinctively Trinitarian Conception of God Among Christians

SIMILARLY TO THE PREVIOUS chapter, let us first very briefly summarize the main tenets of the Christian understanding of God. Because of so much similarity with Islam's doctrine of God—based on the faith in one God of the people of Israel—this synopsis is concise.

In keeping with the foundational belief in one God among all three Abrahamic traditions, Christians are also strongly monotheist. Hence, the one God of the people of Israel, the Yahweh, is the God of Christians, the Father of Jesus Christ. The most distinctive nature of the Christian confession of God is that, rooted in the uncompromising belief in one God of the mother faith, Christianity conceives it as a Trinitarian monotheism, belief in one God as three "persons," Father, Son, and Spirit.

Although the move from the Old Testament to the New Testament without any preparatory notes to the reader may seem almost shocking, with God-talk as Father, Son, and Spirit now pervasive, Christians absolutely reject any idea of "tritheism," belief in three deities. In fact, already in the early centuries, much before the rise of Islam, Christian theologians were compelled to write treatises against Jewish and pagan opponents charging them for tritheism. While it took centuries for Christian tradition to clarify the relations between Father, Son, and Spirit, a consensus emerged according to which each of them is fully God, and that the Father, Son, and Spirit as one is fully God.

Other than the Trinity, Christian theology adds very little distinctive to the Jewish vision of God. The New Testament expands the theme of fatherhood already present incipiently in the older Testament. It plays a far more pervasive role in the New Testament. The God of Abraham, Isaac, and Jacob is the Father of Jesus Christ, and by definition the father of all. This filial relationship shapes the God-world relationship everywhere in Christian tradition.

An important shared part of the vision of God with Israel is the listing of various attributes characteristic of God. On the basis of the biblical narrative and the communities' (people of Israel and the church) experiences, theology seeks to describe the nature and works of God in some coherent manner. A typical distinction is to speak of "communicable" attributes, shared with human persons—such as love, mercy, and patience—and "incommunicable" attributes, unique to God—such as eternity and omnipotence. The big picture of this continuing search is to highlight the infinite goodness and love of God, on the one hand, and the equally infinite power, knowledge, presence, and everlasting nature of God.

In tandem with the mother faith of Judaism, Christian theology believes that while tentative, incipient intimations of God exist widely among various cultures and religions, the mysterious and infinite God can be fully known only by divine revelation. The Christian surplus is that in the person and incarnation of Jesus Christ as one-among-us, we have a full access to the knowledge of God, the Father of Jesus Christ. Although never perfect, let alone comprehensive, the knowledge about God in Christ and Scripture is sufficient for salvation and good life. At the same time, theologians remind us that the finite human mind can only know so much about the infinite.

The Absolute Oneness and Unity of God at the Center of Muslim Faith

While, as mentioned, all Abrahamic faiths are strictly monotheistic, that is they believe in one God, there is no other tradition to which the insistence on the absolute oneness and unity of God would be more central than Islam. While affirmed everywhere in Islamic theology and proclamation, the short sura 112 of the Qur'an puts it succinctly, rejecting also what it takes as the fallacy of the Christian confession of the Trinity:

> Say: "He is God, One.
> God, the Self-Sufficient, Besought of all.
> He neither begot, nor was begotten.
> Nor is there anyone equal to Him."

Hence, the basic Muslim confession of *shahada* states that "There is no god but God, and Muhammad is the apostle of God." An essential aspect of the divine unity is Allah's distinction from all else. The common statement "God is great" (*Allah akbar*) means not only that but also that "God is greater" than anything else. Hence, the biggest sin is *shirk*, associating anything with Allah. Importantly, *shirk* literally means "ingratitude." In other words, "there is only one divine Creator who should be thanked and praised; no other being is to be given the thanks due only to God."[1]

In contrast to popular misconceptions, the term *allah*, which predates the time of Muhammad, did not originate in the context of moon worship in Arabia (even though the crescent became Islam's symbol and moon worship was known in that area). Instead, the term derives from Aramaic and Syriac words for God. In that light, it is fully understandable that even among Christians in Arabic-speaking areas the term *Allah* is the designation for God. That observation, however, does not of course settle the issue of whether Christians and Muslims worship the same God, a theme to be discussed in more detail below.

As everything else in Islamic doctrines and beliefs is based on the Qur'an, it is helpful to very briefly outline the big picture of its teaching on God. As for major themes, along with God's transcendence ("otherness") and mercy, the following are central: first, God as creator and origin of everything; second, the divine unity, mentioned above; and, third, the dual emphasis on Allah's omnipotence and benevolence.[2]

Furthermore, the theme of Allah's justice and judgment looms large in the Qur'an but, similarly to Christian and Jewish traditions, they must be linked with mercy.[3] Echoing the Jewish-Christian teaching, the leading medieval teacher and authority al-Ghazzali reminds us that for God

1. Carman, *Majesty and Meekness*, 323.

2. Gardet, "Allāh," 407.

3. For an important discussion of love, mercy, and justice in relation to Allah, see Volf, *Allah*, 149–86.

"My mercy is greater than My wrath," but that is not a pretext for complacency, as if, "Well, whatever we do, God is merciful."[4]

It is to be noted that the unity and oneness of God, far beyond a mere confession of lips, guides and regulates the whole life and faith of Muslims. The highest purpose life is to honor the unity of God and to willingly submit (*muslim*) to it in obedience and gratitude. The confession lays claim on everything in personal, communal, and societal life.

This fact also helps explain another essential part of Islamic faith, namely its public aspect. God's unity and oneness, as taught in the divinely inspired Holy Scripture, encompasses and guides all of life, not only the spiritual life. "Faith does not concern a sector of life—no, the whole of life is *islam* [submission]."[5] The confession of the oneness and unity of God, the first of Five Pillars of Islam (others being: prayers, almsgiving, fasting, and pilgrimage) shape all of life. Herein, there is of course a radical difference from typical modern Christian settings—particularly in, but not limited to, the Western countries—in which faith is a private matter, kept away from the secular and nonreligious.

When living in a foreign minority position, as all Muslims currently residing in the West do, this life-embracing religiosity of course brings about several challenges. As foreign as it is to the sensibilities of modern Christianity and societies, it would be helpful to try to understand why calls for *sharia*, the Muslim law, are growing.

God Is Known by Many Names!

Even those with only a casual knowledge of Islam may well have heard the expression of "99 Beautiful Names," yet another way to honor and elevate God, the only one. While the Qur'an does not specify ninety-nine names—indeed, more than ninety-nine names and designations of God can be found therein—early in Islamic theology the number ninety-nine came to be used. The Qur'an merely mentions: "to God belong the Most Beautiful Names" (Q 7:180).

A typical list in English includes the following designations: the Beneficent, the Merciful, the King, the Most Holy, the Giver of Peace, the Infuser of Faith, the Guardian, the Mighty One, the Dominant One, the Creator, the Great Forgiver, the All-Prevailing One, the Provider, and

4. Al-Ghazzali, *Alchemy of Happiness*, 32, 41.

5. Vroom, *No Other Gods*, 84.

so forth.[6] Very interestingly, there is no unanimity concerning whether Allah belongs to that number or is the hundredth one. Be that as it may, that foundational name is attached to a number of other designations, for example, *al-Malik* (the King), *al-Salam* (the Peace), and *al-Muhaymin* (the Vigilant).[7]

While the naming of God in Judeo-Christian Scriptures is a common feature, the knowledge, memorization, and recitation of the divine names is even more important in Islamic piety. With this in mind, it is highly significant that all suras in the Qur'an, save one (sura 9) begin with one of the most important names of God, the Compassionate, the Merciful! This observation also reminds us of the uttermost centrality of God and the knowledge and acknowledgment of this One God to Islam.

The naming of Allah, similarly to Christian and Jewish tradition, is linked with what in classical theology is called the attributes of God. They are listing of characteristics and features of God. From the Bible we may recall this familiar listing of the attributes in Exodus 34:6–7 (NIV): "The Lord, the Lord, the compassionate and gracious God, slow to anger, abounding in love and faithfulness, maintaining love to thousands, and forgiving wickedness, rebellion and sin."

While there hardly is a classified typology of attributes in Islamic tradition, the thirteen attributes mentioned in Q 59:22–24 serve as a wonderful example:

> He is God, than Whom there is no other god, Knower of the unseen and the visible. He is the Compassionate, the Merciful. He is God, than Whom there is no other god, the King, the Holy, the Peace, the Securer, the Guardian, the Mighty, the Compeller, the Exalted. Glorified be God above what partners they ascribe! He is God, the Creator, the Maker, the Shaper. To Him belong the Most Beautiful Names. All that is in the heavens and the earth glorify Him, and He is the Mighty, the Wise.

Based on this and some other scriptural passages, al-Ghazali's listing of attributes includes the following: God who is knowing, powerful, living, willing, hearing, seeing, and speaking, followed by four "properties": existence, eternity, unity, and knowability.[8] Anyone even casually

6. My Islam, "99 Names of Allah."
7. Carman, *Majesty and Meekness*, 327.
8. Zayd, *Al-Ghazali*, 65–101.

familiar with typical Christian theological treatises on God will feel like we are walking on the same terrain.

Can There Be a Close and Intimate Relationship with God?

What about the all-too common claim among the Christians not familiar with Islamic faith and spirituality, that Allah is but a distant, "cold," and power-dominating deity with whom no intimate, close relationship can be had? This allegedly is one of the major differences from Christian faith. For justification of this assumption, it is often presented that because of the danger of *shirk*, no anthropomorphic, humanlike descriptions such as the Father or Mother are allowed.

Is that so? In the mainline, it is not. While of course Muslims need to be cautious about applying anthropomorphic designations to Allah, neither are they unknown, including the "face of God" ("whithersoever you turn, there is the Face of God. Lo! God is Embracing, Knowing," Q 2:115) or the "hand of God" ("The Hand of God is above their hands . . ." 48:10). Consider also this Qur'anic statement: The Creator is "nearer to [the human] than his jugular vein" (Q 50:16). Even personal characteristics of Allah are not unknown, though they are not as prevalent as in the Bible.

Al-Ghazzali at times went so far as to say that "God is more tender to His servants than a mother to her suckling-child," attributing this statement to the Prophet Muhammad.[9] Another noted medieval teacher, known for deep spirituality, Ibn Arabi, with a number of highly respected writings on the topic of love and intimate relationship at the heart of Islamic spirituality, said this:

> God ever mighty and majestic says: "O child of Adam, it is your right from Me that I be a lover for you. So, by My right from you, be for Me a lover.[10]

In sum: similarly to Christianity, Muslim theology of God includes the built-in dynamic between the transcendence (otherness) of God, because of his incomparability and uniqueness, and his immanence (closeness) to us. Against typical mistaken Christian intuitions, with his

9. Al-Ghazzali, *Alchemy of Happiness*, 32.

10. Arabi, *Divine Sayings*, 46.

power, uniqueness, and distinction from all that has been created, for most Muslims Allah is also an intimate, protective, personal God.

That said, there is also a need among typical Muslim teachers to honor the otherness of God in relation to that which is created, i.e., all that is not God. In this respect, there is a difference from the idea at the heart of Christian faith, namely that God, through Jesus and the Spirit, lives "in" the human person and the believer abides "in" God. These kinds of ways of expressing intimacy with the divine likely sounds a dangerous idea for mainline Islam; they can be found only among Sufis and other mystics who thereby test the limits of orthodox beliefs.

Having highlighted so much continuity and common basis between the Muslim and Christian conception of, and belief in, God, a question arises whether, in fact, these two traditions worship the same God albeit with some important differences? Or to put it this way: What, if anything, might clearly distinguish these two traditions from each other?

Let us begin with the latter question, namely the doctrine of the Trinity, which dramatically separates Muslim faith from a Christian theology of God. Only after a consideration of this crucial issue, will we be in a place to consider the former question.

Why Is It That the Doctrine of Trinity Is So Very Difficult to Muslims?

The key challenge in the Christian Trinitarian doctrine for Islam, similarly to Jewish faith, has to do with the fear of compromising the absolute unity and oneness of God, the greatest and unforgivable sin. A closely related difficulty has to do with the Christian confession of the full deity of Jesus Christ, the second person of the Trinity (as well as that of the third person, the Holy Spirit). Hence, to no one's surprise, in keeping with the stress on the absolutely unity, the Qur'anic teaching categorically rejects any notion of the threeness of God, and, relatedly, Jesus' deity.

> O People of the Scripture, do not go to extremes, in your religion and do not say about God except the truth: the Messiah, Jesus the son of Mary, was only the Messenger of God . . . So believe in God and His messengers, and do not say, "Three." Refrain, it is better for you. Verily, God is but One God. Glory be to Him, that He should have a son . . . (Q 4:171).

> They indeed are disbelievers those who say, "Indeed God is the Messiah, son of Mary." For the Messiah said, "O Children of Israel, worship God, my Lord and your Lord. Verily he who associates anything with God for him God has made Paradise forbidden, and his abode shall be the Fire . . ." They are indeed disbelievers those who say, "God is the third of three," when there is no god but the One God. If they do not desist from what they say, those of them who disbelieve shall suffer a painful chastisement . . . The Messiah, son of Mary, was only a messenger; messengers passed away before him; his mother was a truthful woman; they both used to eat food . . . Say: "Do you worship besides God what cannot hurt or profit you? God is the Hearer, the Knower" (Q 5:72–73, 75–76).

These texts clearly speak for themselves and call only for brief comments here. In chapter 4 below, a more careful consideration of the many objections to Jesus' deity and incarnation will be considered. Furthermore, as mentioned, it is good to remember that the charge of tritheism (belief in three deities) was leveled against the Christian faith long before Islam. In the fourth century, Gregory of Nyssa had to pen an important rebuttal titled, *On "Not Three Gods."*

A foundational reason for the strict rebuttal of the Christian doctrine of the Trinity in Islam is the sheer absurdity of the idea of God having a child by a woman, a view totally foreign also to Christianity! Often behind the Muslim charge of *shirk* is an inadequate or even heretical (in the Christian estimation) view of who Jesus Christ is, for example that he was a highly elevated divine figure but not equal to God; of course, Christians categorically reject that view as well.

These and other Islamic rebuttals against the Christian Trinitarian conception of the one God are well known and they should be considered carefully. At the same time, there is a mandate for all Abrahamic traditions to work patiently towards a better mutual understanding of the doctrine of God.

Now we are ready to tackle the most foundational question in the doctrine of God among the three Abrahamic faiths and particularly, between Islam and Christianity.

Do Christians and Muslims Worship the Same God?

So, do Muslims and Christians worship the same God or not? This question is not new to either tradition. As early as in the seventh/eighth Christian century, a famous churchman by the name John of Damascus, who had firsthand knowledge of the Muslim faith and who once worked in Muslim administration, delved deeply into this question in the last chapter of his treatise *On Heresies*. Even though he considered Muslims "idol worshipers," John seemed to assume that both traditions worship one and the same God.

Or consider the fifteenth-century Catholic cardinal Nicholas of Cusa who, following the ransacking of the holy city of Constantinople in 1453 by the Ottoman Empire, the Muslim world-power at the time, wrote a highly influential work titled, *On the Harmonious Peace of Religions* (a.k.a. *Peaceful Unity of Faith*). At the same time, he also critically judged Islam's errors! Even Martin Luther, with his well-known and deep suspicions toward Muslims (and Jews), assumed that "all who are outside this Christian church, whether heathen, Turks [Muslims], Jews, or false Christians and hypocrites . . . believe in and worship only the one, true God."[11]

While not often highlighted, it is a well-known scholarly fact that the identification of the Christian and Muslim God—even in the midst of highly polemic debates and mutual criticisms—was by and large the traditional Christian opinion; in that sense, Luther followed tradition. Furthermore, it is the mainstream Muslim opinion that they and Christians believe the one and same God, the God of Israel as is also taught in their Scripture: "We will worship your God and the God of your fathers Abraham and Ishmael and Isaac, One God, to Him we submit" (Q 2:133). That said, Muslims also criticize harshly the Christian conception of this one God as triune and the related claim to the deity of Jesus Christ and the Spirit.

So, what might be the prospects for the future? Despite deep and wide differences in the conception of God, there are also things which uniquely unite them. Both traditions speak of God in universal rather than "tribal" terms. In other words, their message is meant for the whole world rather than to one segment of humanity as is the case, for example with Hinduism and Judaism, albeit differently; neither one of them is a missionary religion in pursuit of converts outside their own flock.[12]

11. Luther, *Large Catechism*, 63.

12. This observation applies even to Hinduism although there are instances of

Similarly to the Bible, the Qur'anic message "is a message for all people: all people should become Muslims, for God is the sovereign God of all people."[13] Part of the universalizing tendency is the important promise in Q 42:15: "God is our Lord and your Lord. Our deeds concern us and your deeds concern you. There is no argument between us and you. God will bring us together, and to Him is the [final] destination." This same sura also mentions that "had God willed, He would have made them one community; but He admits whomever He will into His mercy" (v. 8), and that "whatever you may differ in, the verdict therein belongs to God" (v. 10). Sura 29:46 affirms the same unequivocally: "And do not dispute with the People of the Scripture [but rather; my addition] say: 'We believe in that which has been revealed to us and revealed to you our God and your God is one [and the same], and to Him we submit.'"

Hence, the important reason Muslim theology can unequivocally affirm the identity of the God of Islam and the God of Christianity has to do with the principle of continuity—in terms of fulfillment—between the divine revelations given first to the Jews, then to Christians, and finally, in the completed form, to Muslims

> Say: 'We believe in God, and in that which has been revealed to us, and revealed to Abraham, Ishmael, Isaac, Jacob, and the Tribes, and that which was given to Moses, and Jesus, and the prophets, from their Lord, we make no division between any of them, and to Him we submit' (Q 2:136).[14]

---

outreach to non-Hindus. But they are very limited: some smaller sects outside India and some attempts to reach those few Hindus who have changed their religion into something else in India.

13. Vroom, *No Other Gods*, 104.

14. See also 6:82–90: "Those who believe and have not confounded their belief with evildoing, theirs is security; and they are rightly guided. That argument of Ours We bestowed upon Abraham against his people. We raise up in degrees whom We will; surely your Lord is Wise, Knowing. And We bestowed upon him Isaac and Jacob; each one We guided. And Noah We guided before, and of his seed, David and Solomon and Job and Joseph, and Moses and Aaron; and so We requite the virtuous. And Zachariah and John, and Jesus, and Elias; all were of the righteous. And Ishmael and Elisha, and Jonah and Lot, all We preferred above all the worlds. And of their fathers, and of their seed, and of their brethren; and We chose them and We guided them to a straight path. That is God's guidance wherewith He guides whom He will of His servants; had they been idolaters, all that they did would have been in vain. They are the ones to whom We gave the Scripture, judgement, and prophethood; so if these disbelieve therein, then indeed We have entrusted it to a people who do not disbelieve in it. They are the ones whom God has guided; so follow their guidance. Say, 'I do not ask of you any wage for it; it is only a reminder to all the worlds.'" And 29:46: "And do not dispute with the People of the Scripture unless it be with that, bettering the most virtuous way, except [in the case

While Christian tradition understands the principle of universality differently, essentially it shares the same viewpoint: the God of the Bible, Yahweh, the Father of Jesus Christ, is the God of all nations and the whole of creation.

An important asset to Christian theology for reflecting on the relation of Allah to the God of the Bible is its relation to Judaism. Hardly any Christians would deny that Yahweh and the Father of Jesus Christ are one and the same God. Yet Jews no less adamantly oppose the Trinitarian confession of faith, including the deity of the Son and Spirit. This simply means that Christian tradition is able to confess belief in and worship one God even when significant differences exist in the understanding of the *nature* of that God. To confess one God does not require an identical understanding of the nature of God.

It is important to clarify the many Islamic misunderstandings about what the Christian Trinitarian confession means. What if it is true that "what the Qur'an denies about God as the Holy Trinity has been denied by every great teacher of the church in the past and ought to be denied by every orthodox Christian today"?[15] These include the typical misconceptions among the Muslims, including the inclusion of Mary in the divinity along with Father and Son, the so-called Arianist interpretations which deny the full deity of Christ, and the blunt charge of tritheism. Having affirmed that Muslims and Christians believe in the same God, the Dutch Christian philosopher of religion Hendrik Vroom "would like to add that Christians, on the basis of the gospel, are better *able* to know God than Muslims are."[16] This is not an expression of a puffed-up spirit of superiority but rather a confident call to Muslims from a Christian perspective to consider rich values in the Christian Trinitarian conception of faith in one God. Muslim theologians, in their own terms, would undoubtedly issue the same challenge to Christians.

A Brief Afterthought: At this point, it is wise to continue pursuing the question of the identity of Allah and the Father of Jesus Christ. As Christians we have to learn to live with the lack of total certainty and be willing to listen to both parties in our tradition, namely those who might respond positively to the question of the subheading and those who

---

of] those of them who have done wrong, and say: 'We believe in that which has been revealed to us and revealed to you our God and your God is one [and the same], and to Him we submit.'"

15. Volf, *Allah*, 14.

16. Vroom, *No Other Gods*, 113. Emphasis original.

either reject it, or dare not to take sides. More important than a consensus, let alone full agreement, is to continue conversation and reflection both among Christians and with Muslims about this all-important issue.

4

Why Is Jesus So Important for Muslims?

Jesus Christ in Christian Faith

CHRISTIAN THEOLOGY AND FAITH is focused on the centrality of Jesus Christ. Without him, there would not have been this new religion that at first was considered to be but one of the many Jewish sects. The New Testament takes up the diverse Jewish messianic expectations and applies them to a historical person, Jesus of Nazareth, the Christian Messiah. Unlike in Jewish tradition, in the New Testament the Messiah is not only a divine figure but also deity, alongside the Father and Spirit.

While the focus of the Synoptic Gospels (Matthew, Mark, and Luke) is to present Jesus of Nazareth as a man sent by God to preach and call to repentance in submission to God's will, to heal and restore, as well as to liberate from oppressing powers, the central theme of Pauline and many other New Testament authors is to articulate a more theologically astute description of this God-man. John's Gospel also makes a significant contribution in speaking of the divine Word (*Logos*), an alleged reference to Christ's deity, as having become one of us (John 1:14).

The early creedal statements, in rejection of what came to be determined heretical deviations from orthodoxy, sought to summarize and defend the incipient and narrative Christian theology of Christ in a more formal manner. Notwithstanding centuries-long and still continuing debates about details, the following tenets of Christology are universally embraced by all churches: that Jesus Christ

- is the second person of the Trinity who became truly human in the form of Jesus of Nazareth, and is confessed to be true man (human) and true God (divine), of one "essence" with the Father and the Spirit (without the three being confused with each other or separated, though distinguished from each other);
- was conceived by the Holy Spirit and was born of the Virgin Mary;
- was sinless as totally obedient Son to the Father and by virtue of being divine;
- suffered as the innocent one, died on the cross, was buried, descended into "hell," and was raised to new life by his Father in the power of the Spirit, for our salvation; and
- subsequently ascended into heaven and now rules at the right hand of the Father and will return to establish God's kingdom, the righteous rule, and so help consummate the triune God's eternal purposes.

That said, both throughout history and particularly in the aftermath of the Enlightenment and the ensuing biblical criticism, fierce internal debates have been carried on about all of these and related affirmations. However, these "creedal" convictions (based on various early creeds, confessions of faith) have not lost their foundational meaning, based as they claim to be on the witness of the Bible.

To give a big picture of the contours of the many internal christological debates: whereas Christian tradition represents what can be named "high Christology" with the confession of full deity and humanity of Jesus Christ, the modernist "low Christology" has little use for ancient beliefs in divinity, preexistence, and other Godlike conceptions. Instead, low Christology focuses on the meaning of Jesus Christ as a this-worldly teacher, reformer, and visionary. This bifurcation with many sub-schools has also implications to interfaith dialogues, particularly with Islam and Judaism.

Now to the Islamic conception of Jesus. Whereas it is appropriate and even necessary to speak about "Jesus Christ" in the Christian context, for Muslims it only makes sense to call him Jesus! Why that is so will become evident in the discussion below.

The Islamic Profile of Jesus

Over against a typical misunderstanding among Christians unlearned in Islam, Jesus of Nazareth plays a huge role in Muslim theology and doctrine. The Roman Catholic Second Vatican Council's document *Nostra Aetate* (Declaration on the Relation of the Church to Non-Christian Religions) sums up the general Muslim perception of Jesus: "Though they do not acknowledge Jesus as God, they revere Him as a prophet. They also honor Mary, His virgin Mother; at times they even call on her with devotion."[1] This is an apt description as it both highlights Jesus' and his mother's important role in Islam and at the same time, reminds us of the dramatic difference in the perception and interpretation of who Jesus is.

It is indeed the fact that the main challenge to Islamic-Christian engagement around Jesus Christ is not the lack of interest in Jesus on the Muslim side but rather the somewhat ironic fact that for the faithful Muslim, Jesus of Nazareth plays such an important role! Indeed, one cannot be a true Muslim and ignore Jesus! Counterintuitively, "Islam is the only religion other than Christianity that *requires* its adherents to commit to a position on the identity of Jesus"![2] So much so that it can be said that "[in] the Islamic tradition, Jesus ('Isa) was a Muslim."[3] To many Christians' surprise, one may find book titles such as *The Muslim Jesus*.[4]

There are roughly one hundred references or allusions to Jesus and his mother Mary in the Qur'an alone, and the commentary literature is rich with allusions and references to him. Alongside 'Isa (Jesus), a number of significant nomenclatures are applied to him in the Qur'an, including the

- Prophet (Q 4:163)[5]
- Servant of God (Q 19:30)[6]

1. Vatican Council II, *Nostra Aetate*, para. 3.

2. Barker and Gregg, "Muslim Perceptions," 83. Emphasis original.

3. Meshal and Pirbhai, "Islamic Perspectives," 232.

4. Khalidi, *Muslim Jesus*.

5. "We have revealed to you as We revealed to Noah, and the prophets after him, and We revealed to Abraham and Ishmael and Isaac, and Jacob, and the Tribes, and Jesus and Job and Jonah and Aaron, and Solomon, and We gave to David the Inscribed Book" (Q 4:163).

6. "He said, 'Lo! I am God's servant. He has given me the Scripture and made me a prophet'" (Q 19:30).

- Messenger (Q 2:87)[7]
- Messiah and—astonishingly—even God's "Word" and "Spirit": "O People of the Scripture, do not go to extremes, in your religion and do not say about God except the truth: the Messiah, Jesus the son of Mary, was only the Messenger of God, and His Word which He cast to Mary, and a spirit from Him" (Q 4:171).[8]

These are lofty, highly respected titles and they deserve a more careful look. Furthermore, Jesus is put in the line of a number of Old Testament prophets beginning with Noah, Moses, and Abraham:

> And verily We sent Noah and Abraham and We ordained among their seed prophethood and the Scripture; and some of them are [rightly] guided and many of them are immoral. Then We sent follow in their footsteps Our messengers, and We sent to follow, Jesus son of Mary, and We gave him the Gospel, and We placed in the hearts of those who followed him kindness and mercy . . ." (Q 57:26–27).

Indeed, "Belief in Jesus is one of the major principles of faith in Islam, as he is considered one of the five elite prophets; the others are Abraham, Moses, Noah, and Muhammad, peace and blessings be upon them all."[9]

Although the Qur'an contains nothing like the New Testament Gospel narratives, there are numerous references to key events in Jesus' life, from conception to earthly ministry to death/resurrection to his eschatological future—as much as their interpretation deviates from that of Christian theology. An important reason for differing interpretations is that in the profiling of Jesus in the Qur'an—apart from the strict rebuttal of any notion of his deity (to be discussed below)—there is the reliance on many (Christian and other) legends and other Gospel materials that are not a part of the New Testament canon. Particularly important is the Gospel of Barnabas, whose influence even today is immense in anti-Christian polemics. Hence, with all the commonality, the Islamic description of Jesus is markedly different from the Christian one.

7. "And We gave Moses the Scripture, and after him We sent successive messengers, and We gave Jesus son of Mary the clear proofs, and We confirmed him with the Holy Spirit . . ." (Q 2:87).

8. You may wish to consult Ravi, "References to Jesus."

9. Saritoprak, *Islam's Jesus*, xii.

Similarly to the New Testament, the Qur'anic Jesus is a miracle-worker even if many of the miracles recounted are not known in the Bible, including speaking as a baby from the cradle (Q 19:27–33) and inviting a feast table full of food down from heaven (Q 5:112–14). Most astonishingly, the Qur'an (3:49) testifies that Jesus "will create for you out of clay like the shape of a bird then I will breathe into it, and it will be a bird by the leave of God. I will also heal the blind and the leper; and I bring to life the dead, by the leave of God."

What is astonishing in all of this is that there is not one miracle assigned to the Prophet Muhammad in the Qur'an (although there are in the later traditions); the reason is that his mediatory role in the coming to existence of the Qur'an is the highest miracle. Furthermore, in Islam, any more than, say, in Judaism, the ability to bring about miracles does not make the human person divine.

Jesus' teachings, based largely on the Torah, are highly respected: "From a Muslim perspective, theologically speaking, the essence of the message of Muhammad is consistent with the original ethical and pastoral teachings of Jesus. Any difference is due to the different contexts in which the two men lived."[10]

Unbeknownst to many, Jesus' figure as an eschatological prophet and his awaited return plays a crucial role in Islamic theology. This relates to the dominant role of the expectation of the End in that tradition, even more so than in Christianity (to be studied in the last chapter).

Mary's role is much more prominent in the Qur'anic presentation than in the Bible. Both of the two main suras that contain the most references to Jesus, 3 and 19, are named after Mary. Among about seventy references to Mary, there is also a short family history in these suras; her name is also mentioned elsewhere in Scripture and numerous times in later writings.

> According to the Qur'an, she is not divine but is a servant of God and is chosen above all the other women of the world (3:42). She is not to be worshiped, but she is among the great worshipers of God (66:12). She is a righteous servant of God (5:73) and, along with Jesus, a sign from God (23:50). In most Qur'anic verses that mention Jesus either by name or by his title, the Messiah, he is referred to as "the son of Mary," another indication of her importance for Islam. There are also many references to Mary in the Hadith (sayings of the Prophet). The Prophet on many

10. Saritoprak, *Islam's Jesus*, 4.

> occasions describes her as the master of the women of Paradise. There is an important hadith, which is found in various forms in most of the major, authenticated hadith sources in which Mary is mentioned together with Khadija (the wife of the Prophet), Fatima (the daughter of the Prophet), and Asiya (the wife of Pharaoh) as the dignitaries of Paradise.[11]

A significant reason for Mary's importance is the virgin conception of her son, Jesus. Similarly to the New Testament narrative, Mary's exclaims with great surprise: "Lord, how shall I have a child when no mortal has touched me?" (Q 3:47).[12] That said, we have to hasten to add that the virginal birth of Jesus has nothing to do with Christian claims for divinity; it just denotes a uniquely chosen servant of God.

Jesus Between Muslim and Christian Interpretations

While Jesus matters a lot to both traditions, as even the brief discussion above indicates, a constructive, respectful dialogue about Jesus' meaning and significance has not been on the forefront in the encounters between the two cousin faiths. Even the fact that both the Qur'an and later writings speak so much of Jesus has not facilitated much dialogue until recently. Rather, polemics and mutual condemnations have been the usual tactics. Understandably, the question about Jesus is a sensitive issue particularly in light of Christian claims for his deity. Hence, the topic has garnered apologetics and polemics rather than mutual learning.

In fact, ambiguity and mutual condemnation have characterized Muslim-Christian exchange about Jesus from the beginning—with problems on both sides. On the Christian polemical side, from the beginning of the encounter with Islam, a handful of arguments have persisted, often used in an uncritical and unnuanced manner against any Muslim interpretation of Jesus. These arguments have claimed that the Qur'anic presentation of Jesus suffers not only from mistakes and misinformation because it is based on many sources beyond the officially accepted Christian ones, but that it is also highly distorted and ideological. Christians have also reminded their Muslim counterpart that notwithstanding the Prophet's early more positive attitude towards Christians and the figure

11. Saritoprak, "Mary in Islam," para. 1.

12. See also Q 19:20: "'How shall I have a boy when no human being has [ever] touched me, neither have I been unchaste?"

of Jesus, it is also hampered by many heretical and otherwise suspicious sources. Furthermore, very interestingly, Christians have wondered whether, in fact, some elements of the Qur'anic presentations of Jesus might be more "Christian" than Muslims suppose, including pointers to Jesus' divinity. A good example is the widely debated Qur'anic reference (Q 4:171) to Jesus as the "Word" of God and the "spirit" of God.

The Muslim counterargument, however, has to be fully acknowledged: the very same verse bluntly denies any Trinitarian thought or affirmation of the deity of this "son of Mary."[13] In other words, the foundational Christian affirmation of Christ as the divine "Word" or the (Holy) Spirit cannot be read into the Qur'anic texts. The same applies to the highly honorary title of Messiah given to Jesus—a surprising title in light of the fact that Islam is not a messianic religion in the way the two older Abrahamic traditions are and in that the title is uniquely reserved for Jesus. While it is difficult to determine the exact meaning of Islamic interpretation of the term, it is absolutely clear that it contains no divine connotations in the manner of Christian usage. Whereas in Christian tradition, Messiah, the Anointed One, is integrally connected with the Spirit of God, empowered for his divine ministry, in Islamic tradition the reference to the spirit in the context of naming Jesus the Messiah (in Q 4:171) likely has as its context the creation of human being (Adam: having "proportioned him," God "breathed of My Spirit in him" [Q 15:29]). Again, the importance of differing hermeneutical (interpretive) lenses is at work.

No less different is the interpretation of the narrative of the crucifixion. The Qur'anic explanation for the crucifixion (and incidentally the only explicit reference to it) in Q 4:157–59 reads as follows:

> And for their saying, 'We slew the Messiah, Jesus son of Mary, the Messenger of God.' And yet they did not slay him nor did they crucify him, but he was given the resemblance [or: "but a semblance was made to them"].[14] And those who disagree concerning him are surely in doubt regarding him. They do not have any knowledge of him, only the pursuit of conjecture;

13. "O People of the Scripture, do not go to extremes, in your religion and do not say about God except the truth: the Messiah, Jesus the son of Mary, was only the Messenger of God, and His Word which He cast to Mary, and a spirit from Him. So believe in God and His messengers, and do not say, 'Three.' Refrain, it is better for you. Verily, God is but One God. Glory be to Him, that He should have a son! To Him belongs all that is in the heavens and in the earth. God suffices as a Guardian" (Q 4:171).

14. Alternative translation by Robinson, *Christ in Islam*, 106.

> and they did not slay him for certain. Nay, God raised him up to Him. God is ever Mighty, Wise. And there is not one of the People of the Scripture but will assuredly believe in him before his death; and on the Day of Resurrection he will be a witness against them.

The most common Muslim interpretation of the crucifixion is that Jesus of Nazareth did not die on the cross but that a substitute took his place. As to the identity of the substitute, a number of candidates are listed, usually headed by Simon of Cyrene or Judas Iscariot. Instead of dying on the cross, such interpretations say, Allah took Jesus up to heaven to await his return to earth at the eschaton (to be discussed in chapter 11).

Two key observations from the text are particularly important for our purposes: the meaning of "God raised him up to him" (v. 158) and of "a semblance was made" (v. 157) The former has to do with what really happened to Jesus if he was not put to death on the cross. The latter relates to the question of who, instead of Jesus, was crucified. The main Christian counterargument is that the Qur'an is inconsistent, on the one hand, in affirming the death of Jesus (Q 3:55; 19:33) and, on the other hand, in denying it (Q 4:157). Be that as it may, any interpretation of the events of the cross—even if Jesus might have died on the tree—does not have any salvific or atoning meaning in Islam.

As we continue the work of comparison, let us keep in mind the wise advice according to which "The Qur'an must be explained by the Qur'an and not by anything else" and similarly, the Bible has to be explained by the Bible![15] The urgency of this principle is heightened as we continue comparison about the most deeply dividing issues about Jesus between these two traditions, namely the Christian claim for his deity and incarnation. Here we come to the crux of centuries-long debates, disputes, polemics, and attempts towards mutual understanding without compromising one's own identity.

The Muslim Rebuttals of Jesus' Deity and Incarnation

A contemporary Muslim scholar sets the question of the divine sonship and deity of Jesus in a proper perspective: "Jesus the 'Christ,' the 'eternal logos,' the 'Word made flesh,' the 'Only Begotten Son of God' and second person of the trinity has been the barrier separating the two communities

15. Räisänen, "Portrait of Jesus," 124.

[Muslims and Christians] . . ."[16] This judgment is consonant with Muslim tradition going back to its beginning, and it must be remembered at all times on the Christian side. To the credit of the Christian tradition, several early theologians (after the rise of Islam), such as John of Damascus, showed an extensive understanding of Islamic "Jesusology" and related beliefs. He was also able to carry on learned and useful conversations in the midst of most deeply held disagreements and disputes.[17]

When investigating this issue, let us not forget that, as mentioned above, likely both Muhammad himself and his early followers were robustly influenced by Christian christological views deemed heretical by the creeds and mainline churches. Hence, it is hard to establish exactly how much early Muslim thinkers knew of the details of established orthodox tradition when they began to engage Christian claims about Jesus and the Trinity. Even some Muslim scholars admit that these early Muslims' assessments were hardly informed by a clear knowledge of Christian creeds and teachings.

A further complicating factor here is that Christian tradition did not of course always speak with one voice—even after the defining Council of Chalcedon (451), a major milestone in the development of the christological doctrine. By the time of the rise of Islam, especially the Eastern Christian tradition (Orthodox Church) was deeply divided into different groups and orientations, some affirming, others resisting or revising key Chalcedonian formulae.

The Qur'an contains only a handful of direct references to the Christian claim of Jesus as the Son of God, and, by implication, his divinity—and bluntly denies it: "It is not [befitting] for God to take to Himself a son . . ." (Q 19:35).[18] Allah, the all-sufficient One, has no need for anything (Q 10:68).[19] The Qur'an also denies the idea of sonship because it is seen as linked with Allah having a consort (Q 6:101).

16. Ayoub, "Jesus the Son," 65.

17. For a sample of John's text critiquing Islam and its view of Jesus in a most learned manner, see John of Damascus, "St. John."

18. See also Q 4:171: "Jesus the son of Mary, was only the Messenger of God . . . So believe in God and His messengers, and do not say, 'Three.' Refrain, it is better for you. Verily, God is but One God. Glory be to Him, that He should have a son! . . ."; Q 9:30: "The Jews say: Ezra is the son of God; and the Christians say: The Messiah is the son of God. That is the utterance of their mouths, imitating the utterances of those who disbelieved before [them]. God assail them! How they are deviated"; 2:116; 17:111; 39:4; 72:3.

19. "They say, 'God has taken [to Him] a son.' Glory be to Him! He is Independent. To Him belongs all that is in the heavens and all that is in the earth . . ." (Q 10:68).

Most other standard Christian claims supporting Jesus' divinity fall on deaf ears among the Muslim critics. As mentioned above, the Qur'anic affirmation of the virgin birth of Jesus does not imply any divinity, nor even the linking of Jesus with God's Spirit or God's Word. Neither do miracles make Jesus divine, merely a divinely endowed servant of Allah. At the same time, Islam emphasizes the humanity of Jesus by frequently referring to him as the son of Mary.

In sum: the whole idea of Jesus as divine, as God, and its implication, the Trinity, is categorically denied (Q 5:72–73):

> They indeed are disbelievers those who say, "Indeed God is the Messiah, son of Mary." For the Messiah said, "O Children of Israel, worship God, my Lord and your Lord. Verily he who associates anything with God for him God has made Paradise forbidden, and his abode shall be the Fire; and for wrongdoers there shall be no helpers." They are indeed disbelievers those who say, "God is the third of three," when there is no god but the One God. If they do not desist from what they say, those of them who disbelieve shall suffer a painful chastisement.

In fact, the same sura continues that affirming the Christian belief about the deity of Jesus should rather invoke the person to repentance and seeking Allah's forgiveness (Q 5:74). In sum: the whole Islamic polemics from Qur'an, to Hadith writings, to later teachings unequivocally trump the whole doctrine of the Trinity, as discussed in the previous chapter.

Alongside the rebuttal of Jesus' divine sonship and his deity, strictly denied is also the Christian doctrine of incarnation, God with us. To their credit, early Muslim polemicists and commentators were fairly well aware of the many different interpretations and nuances among various Christian interpretations of the incarnation. Indeed, these early Muslim thinkers often considered the nuances in Christian interpretations (among the various "schools" inside Christian tradition, such as those of the Melkites, Nestorians, and Jacobites, Eastern Christian communities living mostly in Muslim-dominated areas) more carefully than usually happens in contemporary debates.[20]

The Muslim rebuttals of the Christian doctrine of the incarnation of Jesus Christ, as presented in the anti-Christian Muslim literature during the first centuries of Islam's existence, can be classified under two broad

20. A good orientation to these and related intra-Christian christological views is Micheau, "Eastern Christianities."

sets of arguments.[21] First, incarnation is allegedly inconsistent not only with Muslim but also with Christian Scripture. Muslim scholars quoted Qur'anic passages that refute Jesus' divinity (for example the one quoted above: Q 5:72–73) while employing Qur'anic passages that speak of the mere humanity of Jesus such as in Q 5:75: "The Messiah, son of Mary, was only a messenger; messengers passed away before him; his mother was a truthful woman; they both used to eat food . . ." And recall the note above of the frequent identification of Jesus as the *son* of Mary, as opposed to Son of God. As for the Bible, Muslim scholars devoted considerable attention to the sayings that speak of Jesus' humanity, such as his being the son of David and Abraham (Matt 1:1) and that he ate, drank, slept, traveled, rode a donkey, suffered, and died; similarly, his need to pray, his temptations, and so forth were highlighted. On the other hand, Muslim commentators also downplayed and reinterpreted the importance of Christian interpretation of a few passages in which they saw direct claims to Jesus' divinity.

Second, these early Muslim polemicists and commentators argued that the Christian doctrine of incarnation is inconsistent not only with Muslim and Christian Scripture but also with both of their theological teachings at large. On top of this argumentation was the central Muslim idea of *tawhid*, the oneness of God, which by default rejects not only all notions of incarnation (which would lead to the gravest sin of *shirk*) but also the corollary Christian doctrine of the Trinity. *Tawhid* was seen as taught not only by the Qur'an but also by the Bible, especially the Old Testament (Deut 6:4), an essential part of the Christian canon as well.

A related concern among Muslim commentators regarding the Christian claim to the "Word became flesh" (John 1:14) is the incompatibility of incarnation with God's transcendence, affirmed firmly in both faiths. To Muslim sensibilities, the idea of God becoming flesh violates the principles of God's glory and greatness. Furthermore, Jesus' physical conception and birth as part of the doctrine of incarnation were seen as incompatible with both Christian and Muslim teachings. A logical problem here is the exact moment the two natures were united, whether in conception or birth or afterward. In sum: on top of all Muslim concerns and rebuttals of incarnation is that it involves itself in *shirk*, the greatest sin of all, associating with God what should not be associated with him.

21. My exposition here is indebted to my former student, Reda Samuel, "Incarnation."

Although the impasse remains, deepening mutual dialogue is not useless. These deep disagreements between the two monotheistic religions—including the third mother faith—should not be whitewashed, nor ignored even if they continue staying as critical obstacles to mutual understanding. On the contrary, the deep and critical disagreements call for continuing a honest and respectful discussion and dialogue for the sake of mutual learning and understanding. Recall that the ultimate goal of interfaith comparative dialogue is not necessarily convergence, let alone agreement, but rather a mutual learning about what really separates us and what unites. A crystallization of authentic christological disagreements and differing interpretations would be a valuable mutually affirmed understanding, alongside potentially found convergences or similar tendencies.

The last issue in this chapter relates to the question of the comparison between the Prophet, Muhammad, the founder of Islamic faith and the person and work of Jesus Christ, the founder of Christian faith. Can—or should—they be compared with each other? Or is there a way of comparison more useful than between these two religion-founding Prophets?

Jesus as the Prophet Next Only to the Prophet Himself

In the Hadith tradition there is the oft-quoted and highly respectful statement by Muhammad of Jesus: "Prophets are brothers in faith, having different mothers. Their religion is, however, one and there is no Apostle between us (between I and Jesus Christ)."[22] As is well known, Muhammad's own relation to Christianity and Christian tradition in general, especially in the early phases of his career, was fairly positive and constructive. Only later, when internal Islamic disputes and "excommunications" grew stronger, did the Prophet's critical attitude towards Christianity and his desire to distinguish the new religion from the older Abrahamic ones became more urgent.

Because neither the person nor the work of Christ is in any way as central to Islam as it is to Christianity, the Qur'an sets the portrayal of Jesus in a different context. Jesus is put in the line of a number of Old Testament prophets beginning with Moses and Abraham. Furthermore, as mentioned, Jesus' mother Mary plays a much more significant role in Islam, even higher than in Christian Protestantism.

22. *Sahih Muslim*, Book 43, Hadith 190. For sayings clarifying the relation between Muhammad and Jesus, see Leirvik, *Images of Jesus*, 37–38.

It is important to recall that even though Jesus is named a "prophet" in the Qur'an (alongside Muhammad, the "seal of the prophets")—thereby making him the highest and the most unique prophet—neither one is divine. The reason is that unlike Christian faith, which is determined by belief in Christ, Islam is not based on Muhammad but rather on the Qur'an and Allah. In Islam, only God is divine.

Even the fact, mentioned above, that Jesus is a miracle worker (which Muhammad is not), does not imply that therefore Jesus should be lifted up higher than the Prophet of Islam. Rather, the miracles wrought by Jesus are similar to those performed by Moses and other forerunners of Muhammad. The most the miracles can do is to confirm Jesus' prophetic status—they cannot confirm his divinity. Not even the fact that Jesus is described as sinless in Hadith and legendary tradition, whereas it is not quite certain whether Muhammad was without sin (although in the Shi'ite tradition all imams are!), makes Jesus superior to the Prophet. The same applies to the unique naming of Jesus as "Messiah" (Q 4:171), a designation reserved only for him, should not be read according to Christian interpretation.

Rather than comparing Muhammad and Jesus with each other, the closest parallel to Christ in Islamic faith could be found between Christ's role as the living Word of God and the divine revelation of the Qur'an. Christ as the creative eternal Word finds a parallel in the Qur'an as the similar divine power. Here, there seems to be a fruitful platform for comparison: it is the living, powerful Qur'an as the Word of Allah that most closely resembles the Christian claim for the living, powerful Word, *Logos*, as the Word of God. It is yet to be seen where this comparative work might lead us.

The Pakistani-born bishop of the Church of England Michael Nazir-Ali makes the pointed remark that many of the traditional and contemporary Islamic christologies (or jesusologies) seem to find a lot in common with Christian interpretations of Jesus that work with a "low Christology," basically reducing Jesus' significance to his role as a human person.[23] Hence, ultimately, the loftiest status granted to Jesus in the Qur'an is that of the "highest" predecessor of Muhammad—something like the Baptist to Jesus himself. In the long line of the Prophets preceding Muhammad, Jesus is the highest in stature, next only to the Muhammad himself.

23. Nazir-Ali, *Frontiers in Muslim-Christian Encounter*, 25.

Toward a Faithful and Integral Dialogue about Jesus

A tempting way to try to ease the tension between two vastly different portraits of Jesus in these two religions would be to "water down" the New Testament account of Jesus—for the sake of the dialogue. The classic work in Christian-Muslim relations by the late churchman and premier scholar of Islam, Kenneth Cragg, *The Call of the Minaret*, warns against that orientation. Instead, Cragg recommends that for the sake of a genuine dialogue, Christians should present Jesus to Muslims according to the authentic Christian way based on the Gospels and other authoritative writings. This means that Christians are required to present Jesus to Muslims in the fullness of both his humanity and his divinity. "To concentrate only on element in Jesus that Muslims can at once accept is to fail Jesus himself," Cragg asserts.[24] Thus, to be content with only Jesus the prophet-teacher would not do justice to the Muslim's need. On the other hand, "a simple reassertion of the Christian doctrine of Christ will not suffice" either, without a conscious effort to face honestly the difficulties Muslims confront in trying to understand the Christian interpretation.[25]

For a fruitful dialogue to occur, both parties face challenges. Here the recommendation from the Roman Catholic Hans Küng is worth following. He reminds us of the need to acknowledge the difference between Christian and Islamic interpretations. Furthermore, Küng advises Christians not to read Christian meanings into the Qur'an but rather to interpret it from its own point of view: "For the Qur'an, Jesus is a prophet, a great prophet, like Abraham, Noah, and Moses—but nothing more. And just as in the New Testament John the Baptist is Jesus' precursor, so in the Qur'an Jesus is the precursor—and highly encouraging example—for Muhammad."[26] Commensurately, Küng advises Muslims to evaluate Jesus on the basis of the historical sources of the Gospels: "If we on the Christian side make an effort to reevaluate Muhammad on the basis of Islamic sources, especially the Qur'an, we also hope that for their part the Muslims will eventually be prepared to move toward *a reevaluation of Jesus of Nazareth on the basis of historical sources* (namely the Gospels) as many Jews have already been doing."[27]

24. Cragg, *Call of the Minaret*, 258.
25. Cragg, *Call of the Minaret*, 258.
26. Küng, "Christian Response," 110.
27. Küng, "Christian Response," 111. Emphasis original.

The implication that the Qur'an gives a faulty picture of Jesus, however, is a deeply troubling challenge to devout Muslims. It goes way beyond the unwillingness to reconsider one's own interpretative framework. A leading Muslim thinker, the American-based Seyyed Hossein Nasr, in dialogue with Küng, made this point in a most forthright way: "to suggest that the Qur'ān had the wrong Christology makes absolutely impossible any dialogue with Islam. . . . It must always be remembered that for Muslims the Qur'ān, the whole Qur'ān, and not only parts of it, is the Word of God."[28] Against Küng's historical-critical interpretation of Muhammad's prophecy, Nasr says: "One should be very clear on this point and on the role of the Prophet in the process of the revelation of the Sacred Text. It is because of this Islamic belief in the nature of the Qur'ān as the direct Word of God that any consideration of the Prophet of Islam as having learnt this view of sacred history and Christology from Jewish and Christian sources is the greatest blasphemy in the eyes of Muslims."[29]

This is a fitting epilogue to our focus on Jesus of Nazareth, Jesus the Christ, Jesus the Prophet and Messiah, between the two Abrahamic traditions. An honest, open, uncompromising, respectful dialogue and conversation is the way forward.

28. Nasr, "Response to Hans Küng's Paper," 100.

29. Nasr, "Response to Hans Küng's Paper," 99.

5

Whether Science Has Made Obsolete Belief in God as the Creator

Shared Belief in God as the Creator Among the Abrahamic Cousins

EVEN IF SOME DIFFERENCES exist among Jewish, Christian, and Islamic theologies of creation, to be noted below, in their basic outline they are similar enough to be put under one and the same umbrella. All three traditions believe in God, the almighty Creator, who has brought the cosmos into existence and sustains and guides its life from the beginning to the end. Everything derives from and is dependent on God.

The same Creator also guides the creation with the help of the laws of creation he has put in place: "There is no altering (the laws of) Allah's creation" (Q 30:30, Marmaduke Pickthall trans.). There are divine purposes present in creation. While God and world can never be separated, neither can they be equated. God is infinite; cosmos and creatures are finite.

Similarly to the Bible, the Qur'an describes God as the Creator in the absolute sense, that is, as the One who brought into existence that which did not exist "before": "When nothing had yet come into existence, there was the One, the First (*al-Awwal*)," the ineffable one, incomparable,[1] who never perishes (Q 55:26–27).[2] "He is the First and the Last, and the

1. Iqbal, "In the Beginning," 62.

2. "Everyone who is on it will perish; yet there will remain the countenance of your Lord, [the countenance] of majesty and munificence" (Q 55:26–27).

Manifest and the Hidden and He has knowledge of all things. It is He Who created the heavens and the earth in six days, then presided upon the Throne . . ." (Q 57:3–4). In Jewish-Christian tradition, this same idea is known under the term creation *ex nihilo* ("out of nothing").

The Christian surplus and distinction relate to the Trinitarian shaping of the doctrine of God. God, the Father, is the origin of creation. God, the Son, is the agent of creation, through whom Father brings about creation. God, the Holy Spirit, is the life-giving force and energy. As Martin Luther put it using a most delightful picture regarding creation:

> The Father creates heaven and earth out of nothing through the Son . . . the Word. Over these the Holy Spirit broods. As a hen broods her eggs, keeping them warm in order to hatch her chicks, and, as it were, to bring them to life through heat, so Scripture says that the Holy Spirit brooded, as it were, on the waters to bring to life those substances which were to be quickened and adorned. For it is the office of the Holy Spirit to make alive.[3]

Because of God's handiwork, Abrahamic theologians highlight the meaningfulness and purpose-fulness of the divine creation. Muslims often invoke the Qur'anic passage: "Not for (idle) sport did We create the heavens and the earth and all that is between!" (Q 21:16, Abdullah Yusuf Ali trans.). Speaking of the supremacy of Christ, St. Paul locates also creation's purpose in the very same Christ (Col 1:15–16): "He is the image of the invisible God, the first-born of all creation; for in him all things were created, in heaven and on earth, visible and invisible, whether thrones or dominions or principalities or authorities—all things were created through him and for him."

All this is to say that while Islam and Christianity formulate the doctrine of creation somewhat differently, there is no disagreement about the one God being the Creator, creation's origin and goal. This "big picture" has to be kept in mind clearly when more detailed comparison continues.

Interestingly enough, the Qur'an speaks of the created order as *muslim*. The idea behind the term (which means submission) is that one who submits to God avoids disintegration. Creation follows ("submits" to) the laws set up by the Creator. The Qur'an testifies that "to God prostrate whoever is in the heavens and whoever is in the earth, together with the

3. Luther, *Luther's Works*, 1:9.

sun and the moon, and the stars and the mountains, and the trees and the animals, as well as many of mankind . . ." (Q 22:18). Terminological difference notwithstanding, this is not far from the Judeo-Christian idea of God's creation as an orderly, harmonious cosmos praising God, the Creator, and serving the purpose the Creator has set for it.

Similarity can also be found in the shared idea that, as a result, created realities are considered "signs" revealing the Creator (Q 30:22–27):

> And of His signs is the creation of the heavens and the earth . . . And of His signs is your sleep by night and day and your seeking of His bounty. Surely in that there are signs for people who listen. And of His signs is His showing you lightning to arouse fear and hope, and He sends down water from the heaven and with it He revives the earth after it has died. Surely in that there are signs for people who understand. And of His signs is that the heaven and the earth remain standing by His command; then, when He calls you [to come] out of the earth, lo! you shall come forth. And to Him belongs whoever is in the heavens and the earth. All are obedient to Him. And He it is Who initiates the creation, then brings it back, and that is [even] easier for Him. His is the loftiest description in the heavens and the earth. And He is the Mighty, the Wise.

If all creatures are signs, then "it gives humans the impression that God is within us. If God reveals Himself" through all the created beings, "then it is not difficult to get the idea that wherever humans look we can easily feel the presence of God all around and within us."[4] Hence, the study of nature may draw us nearer to God (Q 41:53): "We shall show them Our signs in the horizons and in their own souls until it becomes clear to them that it is the truth. Is it not sufficient that your Lord is witness to all things?"

Does Religion Really Have Anything Useful to Say About the Origins of the World?

As has become clear by now, all Abrahamic faiths affirm the cosmos and humanity as the handiwork of God, the loving and sovereign Creator. Not only Creator, this same God is looked upon also as the Provider and Consummator. From early on in Christian tradition, the sovereign work of the Creator God was highlighted with the help of the idea of creation

4. Özdemir, "Toward an Understanding of Environmental Ethics," 12.

ex nihilo, "out of nothing," a principle shared with Judaism and Islam (although somewhat differently in nuances).

While traditional exegesis took Genesis 1–2 as a more-or-less literal description of both the origins and logistics of creation, having taken place in six days a few thousand years ago, most contemporary Jewish and Christian theologians affirm belief in creation in consonance with the scientific evolutionary theory. According to theistic (from the Greek term *theos*, God) evolution, the Creator is "behind" the coming into existence and evolvement of the cosmos during the past approximately 13.7 billion years. Yet it shares the same central theological conviction: the world is neither self-originating nor self-supporting.

Not surprisingly, it took almost a century for Christian theology to negotiate the religious and scientific explanations—and even nowadays fundamentalist movements oppose or at least struggle with these ideas. On the global Islamic side, there is fierce and vehement opposition to the explanation offered by the evolutionary scientific theories. They are not considered to be compatible with Islamic teaching.

Before going into more detailed explanation, let me hasten to raise a question which can—and should—not be ignored in the contemporary world, namely whether religions have any standing in engaging this issue in the first place. Of all the religious doctrines, whether Christian or Muslim or those of other living faiths, perhaps the most contested one for the secular person—and to a growing number of the religious people as well—has to do with the origins and workings of the vast cosmos. While people in the Abrahamic religious communities speak of the theology of creation, meaning that God has created the world from nothing, very few if any educated people, so the argument goes, really believe it. Theology should stay away from the scientific conversation—if for no other reason than to save itself from public embarrassment. Science is the discipline that tells us how things are in the cosmos. Religion and faith have their own limited domains of knowledge and experience, and, some say, help us cope with the troubles of everyday life and aspirations for the sweet by and by.

But is that a valid argument? Hardly! On the one hand, no credible religious account of how this vast cosmos and its life forms came into being can afford to turn a blind eye to what the sciences have been able to uncover. Christianity and other Abrahamic faiths believe that it is only because of the vast intellectual capacities granted by the Creator God to humanity that scientific work can be conducted in the first place. And after all, it is God's world, the world created by God, that is the object of all scientific explorations. On the other hand, we might also say that no scientific explanation is able to provide answers to the questions of why and by what agency the cosmos has emerged and functions in such an orderly manner. Or, whether creation as such is meaningful or is merely a function of blind accident. These kinds of foundational questions are left to philosophy and religion to seek meaningful answers. In sum: science and theology should continue careful mutual dialogue, keeping in mind their own distinctive—but mutually enriching—domains of expertise.

Because science exercises such a massive role in the contemporary world, both in the West and elsewhere, various attitudes among the religious people and their leaders in relation to science is a useful orientation to the current chapter.

Islamic Struggle with Modern Science

A radical difference in relation to scientific explanations concerning the origins and workings of the cosmos as well as the evolution of human person exists in the Abrahamic camp. So fierce is the opposition among Muslims that it is not uncommon to find fatwas (more-or-less binding legal-religious rulings) on it. What is striking in Muslim countries is that not only a large majority of the general public but also university students and professors strongly and consistently oppose evolution, particularly human evolution. Even among American Muslims, fewer than half accept evolution.[5]

The most important reason for their opposition is the question of the origins of humanity.

Whereas most all Jews and Christians have found a working sympathetic-critical dialogue with sciences, as mentioned, global Islam has not. It is yet to be seen if the openness to science typical of a growing number of believing Muslim intellectuals working in non-Muslim environments, particularly in numerous institutions of higher education in the West, will begin to penetrate Islamic heartlands.

As a way of comparison, suffice it to mention that no other ethnicity can boast so many leading scientists throughout history and in the contemporary world than the Jewish—all the way to Einstein, the

5. According to the 2007 Pew poll, "Religious Differences on the Question of Evolution," only 45 percent of American Muslims embrace evolutionary theory: Pew, "Religious Differences."

inventor of relativity theories, and Bohr, a pioneer of quantum theories. And yet, the Jews entered the modern scientific field relatively late, no earlier than at the beginning of the twentieth century. Apart from some of the most conservative Jews, even rabbis adhere to scientific explanations and do not necessarily see a discrepancy, nor a conflict, between science and their religious understandings. In this, the religious teachers are following in the footsteps of key medieval philosophers such as Moses Maimonides, who was an intellectual giant of his time. As in the mainline Christian tradition, Jews largely embrace the natural sciences, including evolutionary theory.

Christian tradition has come a long way in its attitude toward the sciences. Before the rise of modern science in the aftermath of the eighteenth-century Enlightenment, theology was seen as the queen of all sciences—illustrated in the founding of the most prestigious universities in Europe for teaching the clergy, theology faculty occupying the place of primacy. When this lofty status of theology in academia was totally overthrown with the coming of modern science and critical study of the Christian Scripture, theology faced a massive challenge.

It is noteworthy that Charles Darwin, the famous popularizer of the evolutionary theory (which, though, had initially emerged before him) was no atheist; neither did he consider his theory to deny the idea of the Creator God. While a desire to avoid conflict with religious authorities might have sparked his remarks in the second edition of *The Origin of Species* on the "grandeur in this view of life, with its several powers, having been originally breathed by the Creator into a few forms or into one,"[6] they also point to the possibility of a theistic interpretation of evolutionary ideas. No wonder, particularly in the American context, evolutionism was first cast in a theistic framework and was not at first greatly resisted by the churches. Rather, it was Darwin's interpreters' atheistic interpretation of evolutionary theory that helped emerging evolutionary theory take a decidedly antireligious turn—which soon caused antievolutionist attitudes among the conservatives.

After many ebbs and flows, gradually all major Christian churches have discovered that while there are radical differences between scientific and religious explanations—as the former works necessarily from the perspective of this world and its workings whereas the latter comes to the task from the perspective of divine reality, God—these two do not have

6. Darwin, *Origin of Species*, 490.

to be totally antagonistic. Theologians can learn much from the world God has created by delving into the rapidly growing scientific results and paradigms. Scientists may be challenged and enriched by raising questions of meaning, purpose, and the similar. The Roman Catholic Vatican II's statement *Gaudium et Spes* states that "earthly matters and the concerns of faith derive from the same God" and hence in principle cannot violate each other. This serves as a paradigm.[7]

While there is a segment of global Christianity particularly in the so-called Majority World (Africa, Asia, and Latin America) and among fundamentalist movements in the USA and elsewhere which either strongly opposes or seriously doubts the possibility of a mutual sympathetic-critical dialogue with sciences, it is safe to say that the large majority of theologians and church leaders follow the current mainline tactics of careful mutual dialogue with the scientific community and scientific findings.

As noted, the situation is dramatically different in global Islam. By and large, there is strong resistance towards scientific explanations about creation and creatures, particularly with regard to the evolutionary sciences. Historically this is a counterintuitive stance in light of the fact that, unlike in Judaism, among the Muslims there was once a "golden age" of scientific and philosophical excellence. Furthermore, it is also to be recalled that current Western scientific academia and Christian theology are indebted to Islamic scholars for their translation and introduction of once leading philosophical and scientific writings of those like Aristotle and his school.

As with the Jews, modern science came to Islamic lands no earlier than in the nineteenth century and particularly in the twentieth. For that and other reasons, scientific education is in the process of catching up. No wonder, some leading Muslim scholars lament the status of scientific education at large in most Muslim lands. Virtually none of the main producers of modern science is a Muslim.

Unlike in the West, in Islamic contexts the link between religion and science is tight, so much so that, according to the Algerian astrophysicist Nidhal Guessoum, even current textbooks are hardly much more than "a branch of Qur'anic exegesis."[8] Unlike the Christian tradition (and more recently, the Jewish tradition), the religion-science dialogue is still a marginal phenomenon among Muslims.

7. Vatican Council II, *Gaudium et Spes*, para. 36.

8. Guessoum, *Islam's Quantum Question*, 180.

Generally speaking, the majority of Muslims reject science because of its alleged opposition to divine revelation. On the other hand, Muslims often uncritically embrace the technocratic practical results of Western science in pursuit of equality with Western nations as regards power and competence.

Similarly to Christian fundamentalists, there is also an effort to build a distinctively "Islamic science" based on the authority of the Holy Qur'an and Hadith. The main problem with that approach is the lack of credibility: rather than a critical mutual conversation with, and learning from science, religion is put to do also the work of science.

As a promising sign of progress is the small, albeit currently very small (but slowly growing) group of Islamic scholars and a few religious leaders who are seeking to negotiate between the legitimacy and necessity of contemporary scientific principles and methods while at the same time critiquing the metaphysical, ethical, and religious implications of the scientific paradigm.

God Who Creates, Also Provides for the World

In all Abrahamic traditions, there is not only celebration of what God, the Loving and Mighty, did in the beginning by bringing about this vast cosmos. There is also the celebration of the many ways in which the Creator of the world is also the One who cares and caters for its needs and processes.

The term *providence* refers to God's intentional, loving care, maintenance, and guiding of the cosmos. The theme is so prevalent in the Bible that it is useless even to begin to compile a list of passages. As St. Augustine put it succinctly, "But the universe will pass away in the twinkling of an eye if God withdraws His ruling hand."[9]

In Islamic terms it can be summarized like this: "The Qur'anic universe works with full purpose, harmony, divine guidance, and providence."[10] It is, as Fazlur Rahman puts it, "one firm, well-knit structure with no gaps, no ruptures, and no dislocations. It works by its own laws, which have been ingrained in it by God, and is, therefore, autonomous; but it is not autocratic, for, in itself, it has no warrant for its own existence and it cannot explain itself."[11] Numerous affirmations in the

9. Augustine, *Literal Meaning of Genesis*, 117.

10. Ruzgar, "Chance and Providence," 107.

11. Rahman, *Major Themes*, 3, quoted in Ruzgar, "Chance and Providence," 107.

Qur'an and later tradition sum up a key aspect of that religion: the same God who creates also provides, and his laws stay unchanged and stable, as quoted above: "There is no altering (the laws of) Allah's creation" (Q 30:30, Marmaduke Pickthall trans.).

The Christian way of affirming divine providence is to refer to Christ, the agency and purpose of all God's dealings with the world, as the passage from Colossians chapter 1 cited above affirms; as a result, Paul sums up that in Christ who "is before all things," "all things [also] hold together" (Col 1:17).

Because of this deep and wide trust in divine providence, quite similarly to their Jewish-Christian counterparts, Muslims are invited to do their own part in preserving nature. This is particularly important in the midst of worsening eco-catastrophe. The US-based Muslim intellectual S. H. Nasr has harshly critiqued the technocratic use of nature in the modern West, and on the other hand, has highlighted the spiritual and moral dimension of the ecological crisis.[12] This is fully in keeping with mainline Islamic tradition, which attributes even the environmental crisis ultimately to "the loss of a relationship between humans, the natural realm, and Allah."[13]

Islamic creation theology's foundational idea of creation as "sign" may have immense ecological impetus, as it links all creatures to the Divine. A related ancient Islamic resource is the concept of balance. Similarly to the heavens, which are sustained by divinely established balance, human beings should be balanced, straight, and honest in relation to each other and to nature.

What role and place does creation (nature) have vis-à-vis humanity? According to Muslim teachers, the goods of creation, unlike in modern science, are not meant for consumption by humanity but rather ultimately are meant for God's service. This is of course not to deny the great benefits of natural resources to men and women but rather to put the matter in perspective.

Here there is a bridge to our next chapter. It continues the creation story with the focus on humanity as the image of God.

12. Nasr, *Man and Nature.*

13. Chishti, "*Fiṭra*," 68.

6

Do Muslims Consider the Human Being as the Image of God?

For Orientation: Do All Religions Speak Similarly About the Human Being?

It is clear without saying so that there is a vast difference between the sciences and theology when it comes to speaking about the human being. The same can be said more widely about the difference between secular cultures and religions. But does it mean that basically all religions speak about humanity in similar terms? No, it does not. It is useful for our purposes to highlight briefly the "big picture" regarding the similarities and differences among the religions when it comes to humanity. This also helps better locate and understand the Muslim-Christian comparison and exchange about this issue.

What is common to virtually all religions is that in their teachings and visions of the human person, humanity is more than merely material. Basically all religions affirm a spiritual (transcendent or "otherworldly," as it were) view. This sharply distinguishes religions from the secular (including atheistic) and scientific view often called "naturalism," which means that all that there is, is nature. Naturalism does not allow any kind of real nonmaterial (or nonphysical) dimension that would not directly derive from the material, physical—although, of course mental, emotional, aesthetic, and other such properties are not denied as the secondary form of existence. But these nonmaterial qualities are just derivative from the material and in that sense do not have ultimate reality.

With this universal religious common basis noted, there is a marked difference between religions. To make this big statement manageable and to highlight the distinctive nature of Abrahamic religions, let us divide living faiths under two categories, the Asiatic and the Abrahamic faiths.

At one end of the spectrum of religions are the great Asiatic faiths such as Hinduism and Buddhism. First of all, neither tradition has any kind of doctrine of creation in the sense of Abrahamic faiths. Rather, they speak of emergence or evolvement of the world and all sentient beings therein. While gods and deities play a significant role in Asiatic religions (with the exception of the earliest form of Buddhism), they are not "creators" per se. Rather, in some sense or another, the cosmos is self-generating. Second, while not denying in any way the role of the physical and material, in absolute difference from modern sciences, great Asiatic faiths believe that the only real and lasting aspect of humanity is the spiritual—to the point that the kind of stable personal identity affirmed by Abrahamic faiths is not endorsed, particularly in Buddhism. Therefore, the whole point of the religious-spiritual quest is to seek release from the strictures of the bodily existence and the persistence of lasting "self" (or personal identity). Ultimately, salvation is envisioned as the "extinction" from existence or "immersion" into some kind of nonpersonal "ocean" of transcendent (otherworldly) "emptiness."

Notwithstanding terminological differences and nuances (to be noted below), the vision of the humanity in all three Abrahamic traditions differs radically from that of their Asiatic counterparts. They agree on the idea of the human being having been created by God and fashioned in some sense or another after the Creator. Furthermore, despite internal differences in nuances, all three Abrahamic faiths envision human nature as "embodied soul" or "spirited body," meaning that both the spiritual and the bodily are the handiwork of God and therefore important. They also make human existence finite and thus not immortal. The goal of salvation is neither exit from this world, nor losing one's personal identity, but rather personal and communal life eternally in the presence of God.

Noting above the radical difference between scientific and religious explanations of humanity, suffice it to mention here tentatively that difficulties similar to those related to the origins of the cosmos continue facing global Islam when it comes to the engagement of evolutionary and other scientific views of the origins and evolution of humanity.

What Does the Christian Concept of the Image of God Really Mean?

Christian theology's most significant concept about humanity, the image of God, claims to provide a foundational account of the human person and humanity in relation to the Creator, other creatures, and the cosmos as a whole. This is in keeping with what was mentioned about Abrahamic faiths in general: the discussion of humanity is placed in relation to God's handiwork and God as the origin, source, and goal of human life. Already the first creation story in the beginning of the Bible introduces this major concept (Gen 1:26–27):

> Then God said, "Let us make man in our image, after our likeness; and let them have dominion over the fish of the sea, and over the birds of the air, and over the cattle, and over all the earth, and over every creeping thing that creeps upon the earth." So God created man in his own image, in the image of God he created him; male and female he created them.

This is the shared belief between the Jews and Christians—even in light of the fact that traditionally the Jewish tradition has been more cautious about speaking of us as God's image in order not to transgress against the biblical prohibition to make an image or resemblance of God, the act of idolatry. The only main distinctive feature in the Christian account of the image of God has to do with the overall theological structure stemming from the Trinitarian doctrine of God: Christian theology links the image of God particularly with the Son of God, who is the perfect and "original" image.

But what does it mean to call the human person the image of God? Notwithstanding the scarcity of direct references to the concept of the image of God in the biblical canon—after three occurrences in the beginning (Gen 1:26–27; 5:1; 9:6), the concept itself appears in only a couple of New Testament passages (1 Cor 11:7; Jas 3:9)—it has become an "umbrella" term. It provides a foundational account of the human person and humanity in relation to the Creator, other creatures, and the cosmos as a whole.

Importantly, not only each human person but also the whole of humanity exists as the image of God. This idea enforces and supports the equality of all human beings, including both sexes. As taught in Genesis 1:26–27, humanity has been created as male and female, a reflection of the communion and relationality that Christian theology sees in the triune Creator.

It is important to note that not only the spiritual or mental aspect of the human person belong under the image of God—rather, all of human person and human nature is included. This helps understand the holistic, all-embracing view of the human person in Jewish-Christian tradition.

Because it is impossible to nail down one specific meaning to the term "image of God" in the Bible, Christian theology has wisely embraced several interrelated aspects: there is something in the structure of the human being which makes him or her godlike, such as reason, will, capacity to love, moral and ethical sense, and the like. Furthermore, humanity has been placed in a unique position before God: men and women have been addressed directly and personally by the Creator God. This alone would give dignity and inviolability to each man and woman. No illness or defect, no suffering or torture, can take away the human dignity and value granted by the Creator. Finally, theologians also remind us that while each human person already exists in the state of the image of God, there is also at the same time growth towards whom we will be ultimately. This end-goal can only be seen in Jesus Christ, the authentic and original image of God. While all of us reflect imperfectly the image, Christ is the true(est) image. Hence, likeness to Jesus is the goal towards which Christians are growing and being transformed (2 Cor 3:18).

Very importantly, the first chapter of Genesis also tells us that human beings are made God's vice-regents; they are assigned special tasks such as naming other creatures, and most importantly, they are invited to a personal relationship with God. This special status also brings with it a unique responsibility. Christian theologians affirm that human beings have been given a say and responsibility in choosing to live with or flee from the Creator's presence.

Now, what about Islam? Can this central Jewish-Christian concept about humanity be found therein?

Islam's *Fitrah* and the Image of God

It is interesting to note that the Qur'anic account tells us that the human being is made of clay (Q 23:12–14)—although it includes details unknown and foreign to the biblical narrative. But the point is that the human being is a result of the direct creative act of God: "And We certainly created man from an extraction of clay. Then We made him a drop in a secure lodging. Then We transformed the drop [of semen] into a clot. Then We transformed the clot into a [little] lump of flesh. Then We transformed the lump of flesh into bones. Then We clothed the bones with flesh. Then We produced him as [yet] another creature. So blessed be God, the best of creators!"

Not only that, but the one made of clay is also breathed into by the Spirit of God—another similarity with the biblical account. That said, there is also a detail totally unknown to the Bible, namely that because of the breathing in of the Spirit of God, the angels prostrated before Adam (Q 15:26, 28–30).[1]

> And verily We created man out of a dry [clinking] clay of malleable mud . . . And when your Lord said to the angels, "Indeed I am going to create a mortal out of a dry clay [drawn] from a malleable mud. So, when I have proportioned him and breathed of My Spirit in him, fall down in prostration before him!" And so the angels prostrated, all of them together.

Based on these and related similarities with the Qur'anic teaching about the human being, a Christian might expect the term "image of God" also to appear in the Qur'an. That is not the case—the term itself can be found only in the Hadith literature: "Allah, the Exalted and Glorious, created Adam in His image . . ."[2] The obvious main reason why Qur'an itself does not contain any direct statement about humanity being created in the image of God is that directly associating even humanity with Allah would constitute the fatal sin of *shirk*.

That said, there are expressions that basically come to affirm the idea of what the image of God communicates. The well-known passage of Q 30:30 is important in this respect. And it is highly instructive to see various English renderings to better spell out the meanings of this verse:

> So set your purpose for religion, as a *hanīf*—a nature given by God, upon which He originated mankind. There is no changing God's creation.

> So set thy purpose (O Muhammad) for religion as a man by nature upright—the nature (framed) of Allah, in which He hath

1. In Christian exegesis of Psalm 8:5, there is no unanimity about whether "lower than angels" (or other divine beings) or "lower than God" is the most correct translation. This is easily seen when looking at various translations (all of which usually provide an alternative rendering as well).

2. *Sahih Muslim*, Book 53, Hadith 32.

> created man. There is no altering (the laws of) Allah's creation (Marmaduke Pickthall trans.).
>
> So set thou thy face steadily and truly to the Faith: (establish) God's handiwork according to the pattern on which He has made mankind: no change (let there be) in the work (wrought) by God (Abdullah Yusuf Ali trans.).

The main point of the passage above is that the human person has been created with "a nature given by God [*hanīf*]," which is said to mean "upright" (Pickthall). Interestingly, in the first rendering above, the word is left untranslated as its meaning is difficult to establish. Perhaps something like "faith," alongside "upright," is meant with this term. The related very important concept, translated "nature" (in two renderings above) is *fitrah*. Somewhat similarly to the Jewish-Christian concept of the image of God, *fitrah* has become a kind of umbrella concept. It clearly has resemblance to the image of God in Christian-Jewish vocabulary.

The term *fitrah* refers to "an inborn natural predisposition which cannot change, and which exists at birth in all human beings."[3] Similarly to the image of God, *fitrah* has a number of interrelated meanings, including moral intuitions and religious instincts. It is an innate predisposition, as illustrated well in the oft-cited saying attributed to the Prophet himself: "There is none born but is created to his true nature (Islam). It is his parents who make him a Jew or a Christian or a Magian quite as beasts produce their young with their limbs perfect. Do you see anything deficient in them? . . . The nature made by Allah in which He has created men there is no altering of Allah's creation; that is the right religion."[4] Note that what is translated into English as "true nature (Islam)" can also be rendered as "in a state of fitrah."

Importantly, *fitrah* is also used in the verse cited above (Q 15:29), which mentions that God's spirit was breathed into Adam. This further accentuates the divinely formed and shaped nature of the human being—without in any way violating the strict *shirk* prohibition.

On the basis of this teaching, *fitrah* is universal, not limited to Muslims alone, and is an immutable feature of humanity. Very closely resembling the Christian idea of the innate knowledge of God, it "is the faculty, which He has created in mankind, of knowing Allah." As a result, belief

3. Mohamed, *Fitrah*, 13.

4. *Sahih Muslim*, Book 46, Hadith 34 (the last sentence is a citation from Q 30:30).

in Allah is natural to human beings.[5] Consequently, Islam is at times called *din al-fitrah*, the religion of human nature, that is, religion that is in keeping with natural human instincts—a claim shared by Christian theologians regarding their own tradition.

All three Abrahamic traditions affirm the dignity of humanity on the basis of this unique creative act of God and a unique relation to the Creator as the image of God or as *fitrah*. Just compare these two statements from Islamic and Christian writings, respectively:

> "When any one of you fights with his brother, he should avoid his face for Allah created Adam in His own image."[6]

> "Whoever sheds the blood of man, by man shall his blood be shed; for God made man in his own image" (Gen 9:6).

A common theme for all three traditions is the idea of humanity as God's viceroy on earth. In Islam, the idea of vice-regency is typically described in terms of the "caliph." According to Qur'an 2:30, when God announced to the angels, "Lo! I am about to place a viceroy [*khalifah*] in the earth," they demurred and wondered if God knew the risks involved because of the frailty of human nature (Marmaduke Pickthall trans.)! In response, the Lord taught them how to name the creatures, and that was a cause of marvel among the angelic beings. By extension, key figures such as Noah were appointed as caliphs, God's prophets and servants, in his case taking care of the ark and calling people to follow God's commands and guidance (Q 10:71–73).[7] But not only prophets and other special persons assumed the responsibility for vice-regency: "Lo! We offered the trust unto the heavens and the earth and the hills, but they shrank from bearing it and were afraid of it. And man assumed it . . ." (Q 33:72, Marmaduke Pickthall trans.). This again heightens humanity's unique position before, and relation to, God—while at the same time it

5. Mohamed, *Fitrah*, 16.

6. *Sahih Muslim*, Book 45, Hadith 152.

7. "And recite to them the story of Noah when he said to his people, 'O my people, if my sojourn is too great [to bear] for you, as is my reminding you by the signs of God, in God have I put my trust; so decide upon your course of action together with your associates, then let not your decision be a secret between you; then implement it against me, and do not put it off. But if you turn away, I have not asked you for any wage: my wage falls only on God, and I have been commanded to be of those who submit [to God].' But they denied him, so We saved him and those with him in the Ark, and made them successors, and We drowned those who denied Our signs. Behold then the nature of the consequence for those who had been warned" (Q 10:71–73).

also reminds of the need to obey and trust in the forgiveness and mercy of God when disobedience has taken place (Q 33:72b–73).[8]

In sum: it has become clear that notwithstanding somewhat differing ways of formulating the doctrine of humanity because of scriptural and theological differences at large, there is a basic unanimity between the Christianity and Islam and among all Abrahamic faiths. Clear and radical differences come to the fore when, in the next chapter, we will consider the question of what is wrong with human beings, the doctrine of sin and fall, in Christian parlance.

Before that another topic to finish up this chapter will be taken up. It brings to light some differences due to radically different attitudes towards contemporary science. As mentioned in the previous chapter, Islam has a deep and continuing struggle with evolutionary and other scientific accounts of humanity and its origins. In fact, the idea of the *evolution* of humanity is even more daring to Islamic sensibilities than that of the whole cosmos.

Islam's Struggle with the Scientific Account of Humanity

The evolutionary line of modern *Homo sapiens* from the closest predecessors, the hominids whose history goes back to about five million years in the past, is well-known and well-documented in current scientific literature. Notwithstanding some important developments in their capacity, even the closest hominid species to modern humans (from about 400,000/200,000 years ago) were vastly different from us, with almost nonexistent progress in the use of tools, lack of artistic skills, vastly inferior mental skills, and so forth.

Briefly stated: modern humans, having been around no more than about 50,000 to 150,000 years, are a unique species. Decisive in the transition to humanity was "that human consciousness and intelligence emerged, and with it creative, artistic, and religious imagination."[9] Hence, to speak of humans as "developed apes" does not make sense from the scientific perspective!

8. "Lo! he hath proved a tyrant and a fool. So Allah punisheth hypocritical men and hypocritical women, and idolatrous men and idolatrous women. But Allah pardoneth believing men and believing women, and Allah is ever Forgiving, Merciful" (Q 33:72b–73, Marmaduke Pickthall trans.).

9. Van Huyssteen, *Alone in the World*, 64.

As much as this evolutionary account differs in "logistics" from the traditional Abrahamic six-day sudden creation narrative, including the creation of "ready-made" first humans, Jewish and Christian theologies with the exception of a dissenting fundamentalist minority have been able to find reconciliation with sciences as long as theistic evolution is followed. Therein, the slow emergence of humanity as rational, emotional, ethical, religious, and self-conscious species is the function of the almighty and loving God guiding the "natural" process of evolution. Here, there is a radical difference from the atheistic-naturalist scientific account, which categorically rejects any idea of divine agency (and even the existence of any divine Agent!). At the same time, there is also a stark difference from the rebuttal of scientific explanations in Christian fundamentalist and global Islamic mainstream communities.

As mentioned, alongside the rebuttal of the evolutionary account of the cosmos and life, in Islam there is a vehement opposition to the scientific accounts of the emergence of humanity. To be precise: there is even a stronger push against any notion of the evolution of humanity in regard to its origins. "There is no doubt that the idea of biological evolution constitutes a major cultural blockage in the Muslim world today," says a leading Muslim scientist, Algerian astrophysicist Nidhal Guessoum, who himself represents a tiny majority of evolution-friendly scholars outside European and North America-based Muslims.[10] Not only do the great majority of people in Muslim countries strongly oppose evolution, but so does the academic elite![11] As mentioned, fewer than half of American Muslims accept evolution at large. The most important reason for opposition is the question of Adam. For religious leaders, the idea of pre-Adamic species is still totally unacceptable.

What is highly noteworthy, however, is that according to some Muslim experts, Muslims have not always resisted evolution, as long as a theistic framework was in place. During the classical "golden era" (the ninth to twelfth centuries), intense debates about evolutionary-kind of ideas were carried on that resulted in an embrace of evolutionary principles "before evolutionism."[12] Even in the debates immediately after the publication of Charles Darwin's main works in the nineteenth century,

10. Guessoum, *Islam's Quantum Question*, 273.

11. This paragraph and the rest of this section is a repeat (with only a few minor changes) from my *Creation and Humanity*, 236–37.

12. Ziadat, *Western Science*, 25.

for a while a diversity of views were entertained, until a total rejection became the normal position.

Currently the only Muslim scholars or religious teachers who advocate evolutionary theory are located in the United States or Europe. Among the very tiny group of scholars who reside in traditional Muslim lands and defend evolution, a leading voice is currently the above-mentioned Guessoum, who teaches in the United Arab Emirates. His 2011 *Islam's Quantum Question* is a highly sophisticated advocacy of evolutionism and an honest self-criticism of the state of scientific enterprise in Muslim lands. He argues that passages can be found that could be interpreted in an evolutionary manner, such as the following:

> ". . . verily He created you in stages?" (Q 71:14).
>
> "It is He Who created you from clay; then He decreed a term [or era]" (Q 6:2).
>
> "When your Lord said to the angels, 'Indeed I am about to create a human being out of clay. So when I have proportioned him, and breathed in him My spirit, then fall down in prostration before him!'" (Q 38:71–72).

It is yet to be seen how and when the global Muslim community may be willing to take up the issue of evolutionism and reflect on its implications for views of humanity—and what, if any, implications that might have to the interfaith dialogue and mutual exchange. We have to keep in mind that neither the reference to history (about the openness to the idea of evolution among the intellectuals in the distant past), nor the singling out one prominent progressive intellectual (Guessoum), represents any kind of sea-change in the big picture of total rejection of the scientific account of the emergence and development of humanity in global Islam.

In the meantime, let us continue the discussion of humanity between the two cousin faiths by turning to the question of what is wrong with us, namely sin and the fall, to use Christian vocabulary. Here again, sharp differences emerge despite such a wide convergence about the origin and nature of the human being as God's image or *fitrah.*

7

What About Sin and Fall?

Human Misery and Sinfulness According to Christian Faith

WHAT THE CHRISTIAN THEOLOGIAN Reinhold Niebuhr wittily observed is undoubtedly affirmed by other Abrahamic traditions as well, namely that the sinfulness of humanity, while a religious claim, is "one of the best attested and empirically verified facts of human existence!"[1] Ironically, it is also here that the agreement among Jewish, Christian, and Muslim theologians stops when it comes to the explanations about whence sinfulness and what is its nature and results. Therefore, with this topic it is particularly important to begin the chapter with a brief outline of the distinctively Christian position. As closely aligned as Christian position about humanity at large might be with other Abrahamic views, ironically, it also deviates radically not only from Muslim theology but also from the mother faith Judaism.

The distinction of the Christian theology of sinfulness is best understood by comparing it first with the Jewish view—both of them allegedly based on the very same scriptural writings! Jewish theologians contend that the Genesis 3 story contains "no doctrine of the fall of the race through Adam, of the moral corruption of human nature, or of the hereditary transmission of the sinful bias," all features of the traditional mainstream Christian understanding (particularly in the Christian West,

1. Niebuhr, "Sin," 349.

that is, Catholicism and Protestantism).[2] In Jewish tradition, Adam plays no role in the rest of the Old Testament story. It also rejects his immortality before the fall.

Instead of original sin, the Jewish (rabbinic) tradition speaks of two tendencies or urges in every human being, namely, for good and evil (*yetzer ha tov* and *yetzer ha ra'*, respectively). Even though the "inclination" to evil in itself is not evil, it is a matter of which of the two is the guiding force in life. Hence, the main term for repentance from evil is *teshuvav*, literally, "turning."[3] Every human being is engaged in a constant fight between the two urges.

This is not to undermine the seriousness of the sinful tendency. Just think of how radically Genesis speaks of the wide diffusion of moral evil in chapters 4–11. In fact, according to the biblical testimonies, human wickedness is great, and even the imaginations of the heart are evil (Gen 6:5; 8:21). In other words, the evil urge is present at birth. But each person is responsible for sinful behavior; such responsibility is not inherited. Although the evil inclination plagues the human person, it neither robs the person of all moral integrity nor causes lostness, as in Christian tradition. It is of utmost importance for Judaism to affirm the freedom from depravity and innate evil of human nature despite the serious inclination toward evil. Second Baruch (54:15, 19; 19:3; 48:42–43; 59:2) teaches that even after Adam's sin, which brought about death, each new generation has to choose their own path. This much can be said in general about traditional interpretation in Judaism. It is clear that there is no lack of debates and nuances throughout history; but for the sake of our purposes, this much suffices.

Christian theology's explanations concerning the origin, nature, and outcome of sin differ drastically from the mother faith's view. The human being is not only in a state of deviation from original innocence but also "fallen" and corrupted. Under the tutelage of former Jewish rabbi Saint Paul, the apostle, Christian tradition speaks of the fall (of Genesis 3) as the origin of sinfulness. Even when, in modern theology, the narrative of Genesis 3 is generally considered a sacred myth rather than a historical story, the fall's effect is nevertheless a reality to be reckoned with.

That said, Christian theology itself does not have a unified account of sin and the fall, despite the universal affirmation of the presence of

2. Cohon, *Essays in Jewish Theology*, 220.

3. Jacobs, *Jewish Theology*, 243.

sinfulness. In Western Christianity (Roman Catholicism, Protestantism, including Free Churches, and Anglicanism), the fall plays a significant role as the backdrop for sinfulness, leading to divine judgment apart from God's grace. Some Western theologians even use the concept of "total depravity," a stark account of the influence of the fall. Yet, that does not eradicate the image of God. Notwithstanding differences in nuances, most Western churches teach the transmission of sin from generation to generation. Although Roman Catholics consider fallen humanity lost apart from grace, in their understanding the capacity to choose between evil and good is not totally lost.

The less negative interpretation of sinfulness is that of the Eastern Orthodox church, in which the fall narrative is depicted as a "stumbling" of yet-immature children (Adam and Eve). While of course a sad experience, the fall did not bring about original sin and certainly not divine judgment. Rather, judgment comes only as a result of wrong choices and acts. The effects of the fall are understood more in terms of a wound inflicted in our nature. Eastern theology also insists on the freedom of will to choose between evil and good. Yet, even there it acknowledges sinfulness.

That said, notwithstanding many debates among the Christian traditions concerning the interpretations of "fall" and "original sin," there is no denying the simple fact that while "no religious vision has ever esteemed humankind more highly than the Christian vision," no other tradition has also "judged it more severely."[4] In other words, as many challenges as we may have in the third millennium in speaking about the "logistics" of what has gone awry and why with humanity, the fact that we are sinners is in no doubt in Christian understanding. The acknowledgment of sinfulness leads all Christian churches to reject salvation by human means; only God through grace is able to save; that is the foundational and radical difference from both Judaism and Islam.

Positive and Realistic Outlook on Human Nature in Islam

In Muslim outlook, somewhat similarly to Judaism—and, perhaps, even more robustly—the human person, while not perfect in any way, is neither fallen nor corrupted. The general assessment of humanity is markedly more positive than among the Christians.

4. Jewett and Shuster, *Who We Are*, 57.

That said, the general Islamic view of humanity is realistic, acknowledging many limitations and even failures of human nature:

- "man is verily a wrong-doer and unthankful" (Q 14:34), the latter being one of the cardinal sins in Islam indicating that he or she has not really fully submitted.
- "he is disputatious, openly" (Q 16:4).
- "Truly he is a wrongdoer, ignorant so that God may chastise the hypocrites, men and women, and the idolaters, men and women . . ." (Q 33:72–73).
- "man was created weak," manifested in that there are "those who follow their passions, [and] desire that . . . [they] deviate with a terrible deviation" (4:28, 27).
- the human person forgets to turn to God as soon as he or she has been rescued from a danger (Q 10:12[5]).
- "among people there are those who dispute concerning God without any knowledge or guidance or an illuminating scripture" (Q 31:20).
- "mankind is ever hasty" (Q 17:11) and "Indeed man was created restless" (Q 70:19).
- (17:11; 33:72; 70:19; etc.)

This short list of the examples that the Qur'an mentions about limitations, sins, and failures teaches us three things. First, they assure us that the positive outlook on humanity does not turn a blind eye to typical negative features and inclinations associated with human beings. Second, it also tells us that the "list of sins" hardly amounts to any kind of "mortal" sins, that is, sins leading to judgment and death beyond the human capacities to repair; that said, there is the well-known listing of seven grave sins, to be discussed below. Third, even when some limitations are such that they go back to the creative work of God, there is absolutely no idea of a corrupted or fallen nature resulting in divine condemnation.

The main reason why even the limitations do not trump the foundational conviction of the goodness (or, at least, the moral neutrality) of

5. "If misfortune should befall a man, he calls upon Us on his side, or sitting or standing; but when We have relieved him of his misfortune, he passes on, as if he had never called upon Us because of a misfortune that befell him. So is adorned for the prodigal that which they do" (Q 10:12).

the nature of humanity is the principle of *fitrah* discussed in the previous chapter. It elevates the human person to a unique place among the creatures. A number of sayings point to this divinely given status.

- "Verily We created man in the best of forms" (Q 95:4).
- "And He formed you and perfected your forms, and provided you with [all] the wholesome things . . ." (40:64).

All that said, the Islamic tradition never envisioned Adam and Eve in terms of perfect paradise imagery after Christian tradition. Again, its account of humanity is realistic, as illustrated in Qur'an 95:4–6: "Verily We created man in the best of forms. Then, We reduced him to the lowest of the low, except those who believe and perform righteous deeds, for they shall have an unfailing reward." That said, in sum: according to mainline Muslim teaching, human nature is, generally speaking, good—or, at least, it is not sinful and corrupted, as in Christian teaching.

Neither Fall, Nor Original Sin

Although Islamic tradition, similarly to others, has had internal debates, particularly with regard to the presence or lack of evil inclinations, the normal Islamic theology assumes a more or less neutral view that takes the beginning of human life as a blank slate, thus emphasizing the role of free will—not unlike in Christian Pelagianism.[6] As established above, the mainline teaching in tradition and contemporary Islamic theology is by and large a "positive view" of human nature.

Unbeknownst to those unfamiliar with Islam, the fact that the Qur'an does not know the doctrine of original sin or the idea of moral depravity does not mean that the fall narrative familiar from the Old Testament would not be a part of their Scripture. Yes, it is. And, even more surprisingly: it can be found in no less than three narratives (Q 20:115–27; 7:10–25; 2:30–38). But its implications (like in Jewish interpretations) differ dramatically from those of Christian theology. Whatever weaknesses the fall brought about, the idea of the lostness of humanity because of sin after Christian interpretation is totally missing (without denying the otherwise negative results of disobedience). The

6. Pelagianism was labeled heretical by a majority of Christians, following St. Augustine, because it seemed to teach that the human person is not innately sinful, nor corrupted, and therefore is able to reach salvation by his or her own efforts and merits.

closest parallel to the idea of "lostness" is the ignorance of the right way and unwillingness to submit to Allah, acts that are conscious choices.

In the (chronologically) earliest narrative (20:115–27), after becoming forgetful of the covenant, all angels were invited by God to prostrate themselves before Adam, and they did, but Satan (named Iblis), who then promised to take Adam and Eve to the tree of immortality and knowledge, declined. They ate the fruit, became ashamed, and tried covering themselves with leaves. "And Adam disobeyed his Lord and so he erred" (v. 121). God called Adam again and advised him to leave the garden that had now become an "enemy" (obviously because Satan was said to be there, v. 117). God promised to guide the human or else blindness would follow for the one who previously was able to see. The punishment of blindness would be revealed on the day of resurrection, and even more severe forms of punishment might follow.

The later account in 2:30–38 repeats very closely the Genesis 3 story with only a few significant deviations. The third major passage, 7:10–25, speaks of the disobedient nature of Adam in starker terms and also mentions his leaving the garden in more certain terms (v. 27). Furthermore, all the accounts speak of enmity and distress as a result of the disobedience for which Adam himself (rather than Satan or Eve) is mainly responsible (albeit tempted and lured by Satan).

In sum: Notwithstanding the acknowledgment of sinfulness of humanity due to its own bad choices, what is totally missing in Islamic theology of sin is the idea of transmission of "original sin" from one generation to another and its punitive effect on the progeny. Adam (along with Eve and Satan) himself is to be blamed for disobedience, not later generations. Importantly, the Qur'anic narrative does not link the fall with lostness, as does Christian tradition.

Can Human Persons Freely Choose the Right or the Wrong?

As has become clear by now, an important corollary issue behind theologies of sin and the fall is the question of the freedom of the will. Recall that even in the Christian camp, there is no total agreement about this vital issue. Whereas in the Christian East freedom of the will was not negated by Adam's disobedience, the Christian West, following Augustine, denies the power of choice apart from divine restorative grace (except for freedom to choose wrongly!).

The freedom of will or lack thereof raises the obvious question about the role God plays in the course of human life and choices. As soon as the religious person denies the freedom of will, the implication is that all that happens is not only foreknown by God but also divinely determined. St. Augustine, who denied the freedom of the will following the fall, also happened to be known for emphasizing divine omnipotence, and even "double predestination" (that is, some are chosen by God for salvation and others to damnation). Not surprisingly, he was confronted by his interlocutors to whom these two ideas would seem to make human sin a necessity, particularly because of lack of the power of will! As much as Eastern Christianity opposes this Augustinian legacy, it is still dominant in mainstream Catholic and Protestant theology.

Both mainstream Judaism and Islam avoid this conundrum by rejecting the Christian-type of teaching about such weakness of will, which totally obliterates capacity to choose between good and evil. That said, although Islam by and large affirms human freedom, not surprisingly there are different schools of thought when it comes to its implications. From the comparative perspective, it is useful to take a brief look at the internal Muslim debates.

The oldest Muslim view tended to be predestinarian in orientation. It applied the cause-and-effect relation evident in creation to human actions as well and attributed both right and wrong to Allah. In many ways, this currently marginal Islamic view resonates with the stricter deterministic interpretations of Christian tradition after the long line of Augustinian reasoning. The "neutral" view came to the fore after the mid-eighth century. Rather than divine determinism, God's justice and fairness came to the forefront. This school interpreted the ambiguous Qur'anic passage, "And God brought you forth from the bellies of your mothers while you did not know anything" (Q 16:78), to mean that the newly born infant is like a blank slate, devoid of either good or evil. Only in the course of growth does either inclination take over. The neutral hermeneutics thus put an emphasis on free will and its implications. This view, then, shifts toward what in later tradition became a highly influential Muslim interpretation, the "positive" view, which basically takes *fitrah* as a state of intrinsic goodness. For that mainline Islamic tradition, two foundational affirmations must be held in balance: belief in the sovereignty of God and his power behind everything that happens in the world.

A Summative Comparison

Because of the great importance of this chapter's topic to any engagement between Islam and Christianity, not the least with regard to the question of salvation, it is useful to summarize and conclude our discussion with a somewhat schematic comparison. We are greatly helped here by a ten-point description listing of the main facets of Islam's view of humanity and human nature as well as what, if anything, is wrong with us.[7] In many ways this comparison also serves as a summative conclusion to both the previous and the current chapter.

1) *Adam and Eve Stumble but Don't Fall.* "What happened in the garden was a 'fall,' but not the 'Fall'" after Christian tradition, rather like a mistake. Rather than Adam's disobedience alienating him from God, in his mercy God forgave him after repentance (Q 2:24–37). "Moreover, Muslims claim it was God's plan from the beginning to put Adam and Eve on earth; it was never to leave them in the garden. The garden was only a training ground to reveal his continual need for the guidance provided through divine revelation."
2) *No Original Sin.* Although humanity is prone to sin, as discussed above, there is no hereditary, innate sinfulness, let alone corruption after the mainline Christian interpretation. Muslims also point to those biblical passages such as Ezekiel 18:20, which place the responsibility for wrong deeds for the person himself or herself. Or else, God's justice and righteousness would be violated.
3) *Everyone Is Born Pure.* Having been born "as *fitrah*: a state of intrinsic goodness . . . people are born pure and sinless. They are Muslims by birth, and salvation is intact, but they must do all in their power to maintain this status." This is a radical and foundational difference with Christianity.
4) *All Have Sinned.* The state of *fitrah*, as discussed above, does not mean sinlessness—except for Jesus whose sinlessness Muslims endorse with Christians. It is just that sin's nature, effects, and outcome are differently interpreted when compared to the Christian tradition.

7. Castor, "10 Things," paras. 1–11. All direct citations come from the same page (unless otherwise indicated). The ten rubrics are not put under citation marks but rather italics have been added in order to highlight them.

5) *God's Law Is Somewhat Arbitrary.* The reason it is at times difficult, or even impossible, to know exactly what is right and lawful as opposed to wrong and illegal is that "[n]othing is right or wrong by nature, but becomes such by the fiat of the Almighty. What Allah forbids is sin, even should He forbid what seems to the human conscious right and lawful."[8] While Christians do not dispute the difficulty of many ethical and moral judgments, in the mainline, they believe that enough has been revealed in Scripture to help the sincere seeker to be able to find the correct answer.

6) *God May Overlook Some Sins.* Allah may overlook some sins if prayers and prescribed ritual purity rites are conducted. God may even hide some sins. While such is not totally unknown in the Christian tradition, it would rather speak of God willing to forgive all sins, small and big, to the one who repents and relies on God's mercy.

7) *Seven Grave Sins* include: *shirk*, magic, murder, usury, despoiling orphans, fleeing from a battle, and false charges of adultery. While this listing differs quite a bit from various Christian listings of grave sins, the idea of making a distinction between smaller and bigger sins is similar. The most well-known such distinction is the Roman Catholic official teaching between venial and mortal sins, the latter resulting in condemnation unless forgiven: lust, gluttony, avarice, sloth, anger, envy, and pride.

8) *Man's Chief Problem: Forgetfulness.* "Disobedience is not rebellion against God but rather a failure to remember His instructions. Satan's goal is to make us forget his guidance (58:19; 20:115)."[9] The Prophet and prophets were sent to teach about the right path.

9) *Man's* [sic] *Sins Against Himself.* With reference to passages such as Q 7:23, "Our Lord, we have wronged ourselves," Castor reminds us that in Islam "sin is mostly against oneself—not against God." He quotes Phil Parshall, a well-known missionary-missiologist: "It is difficult to communicate the biblical meaning of sin to a Muslim. His outlook is horizontal rather than vertical. Often the key

8. Zwemer, *Moslem Doctrine*, 51.

9. "Satan has prevailed upon them, and so he has caused them to forget the remembrance of God . . ." (Q 58:19); "And We made a covenant with Adam before, but he forgot, and We did not find in him any constancy" (Q 20:115).

criterion of a definition of sin is whether or not a person is caught."[10] Although Christian tradition is in agreement about sin violating the sinner as well as other human beings, essentially any sin is against God. Well-known is King David's admission after having been caught in adultery and subsequent killing of the woman's husband: "Against thee, thee only, have I sinned, and done that which is evil in thy sight" (Ps 51:4).

10) *No Mediator for Sin.* Here we come to the most foundational and radical difference between the two faiths: whereas in Christianity salvation and forgiveness is founded in the work and mercy of the Mediator, the Lord Jesus Christ and his salvific work on the cross and in resurrection, in Islam every person is ultimately responsible for his or her destiny. While this is not to deny the graciousness and mercifulness of Allah, Allah is not Savior in the same sense Jesus Christ is. Astonishingly, Castor reminds us that even the Prophet himself was found to be desperate about his and his family's eternal destiny!

This comparative list and particularly its last point is a fitting gateway to the next chapter, whose theme is salvation (to use Christian parlance) or submission (in Islamic terminology).

10. The citation is incorrectly listed on the website but comes from Parshall, *Muslim Evangelism*, 97.

8

If Jesus Is Not the Savior in Islam, Whence, Then, Salvation?

Radically Differing Visions of Salvation

ALONGSIDE THE DRAMATICALLY DIFFERING interpretations of sin and fall, the question of salvation—named submission in Islam—is the other deeply dividing issue between Islam and Christianity. For the sake of a hospitable and respectful mutual dialogue, this difference should not be unduly softened, let alone ignored. Delving deeper into its background and details further helps mutual understanding.

To help envision the big picture, here are the three radically differing orientations among the Abrahamic traditions between Christianity on the one side and Judaism and Islam on the other:

- Whereas in neither Judaism nor in Islam salvation—named redemption and submission, respectively—comes ultimately from God but rather from the best efforts of the human person in obedience to God and the Holy Scripture, in Christianity salvation comes only from the triune God through the atoning work of Jesus Christ. This emphasis on salvation as the work of the triune God does not mean negligence of the pursuit of holiness, obedience, and neighborly love. It is just to say that these good works are rather considered as consequences of the salvific gift and grace.

- With regard to the way of "salvation" in Judaism and Islam, the emphasis on human initiative and response is not to undermine, nor deny, the gracious and merciful nature of God nor claim that God has nothing to do with salvation. It is just to say that in Judaism neither the awaited Messiah, nor even Yahweh, or in Islam, neither Allah, nor his Prophet, is the Savior. God's role is to send revelation and messengers who help guide the Jew to the obedience to the Torah ("Bible" and Law) and the Muslim to submission (*muslim*) to Allah.
- Whereas in neither Judaism nor in Islam there is any mediator of salvation, in Christian theology the work of Jesus Christ as the suffering, dying, and resurrected Savior is the source of salvation. The triune God became incarnate, truly human in Jesus Christ, who lived, ministered, suffered, and died for our sins, and in his glorious resurrection gained victory over judgment and death.

Having now set the background and framework, as with many other chapters, let us first provide a short synopsis of the Christian understanding of the source of salvation in the work of Jesus Christ. This will prepare us for considering the Muslim counterpart's vision of "salvation" and its consistent rebuttals of the Christian salvific narrative.

Christian Theology of Atonement and Salvation in an Outline

The traditional Christian term used to refer to what Jesus Christ—sent by his Father for the salvation of humankind, in the power of the Spirit—has done to bring about reconciliation between God and humans, as well as among men and women, is "atonement." Not without reason, traditional "atonement theories," as they have been called, focus on the suffering, death, and resurrection of the Son of God, without which no Christian account of salvation can be had. Furthermore, incarnation, the "assumption" of human life and its cleansing and sanctification by the Son of God, is also stressed, as well as the resurrection and ascension of Christ.

Broadly speaking, the Eastern (Orthodox) churches highlight the importance of incarnation as well as resurrection and ascension, whereas Western Christianity (both Protestant and Roman Catholic) has focused more on suffering and the death on the cross. For the former, the biggest problem of humanity has to do with mortality, or to put it positively, the possibility of gaining life eternal in communion with God. For the latter, the greatest atonement effect has been in defeating the effects of sin and the fall, namely, the corruption, guilt, and judgment that result in condemnation apart from atonement. That said, wisely enough, the church never endorsed only one of the many atonement theories but rather, let me stand side by side. The most important motifs and orientations behind these many atonement explanations include the following:

- In assuming humanity (incarnation), Christ cleansed and sanctified the course of human life gone awry because of sin and mortality.
- Christ "fooled" the Satan in rescuing humanity as the opponent of God who believed that humanity belongs to him.
- Christ's innocent life and death on the cross satisfied the righteous demands of God regarding the effects of sin.
- Christ's self-sacrificing life and service sets an everlasting example for men and women to emulate.
- The suffering and the cross helps pay the penalty of death and judgment due to sin.
- Christ's resurrection and death opens the way for mortal humanity to have life eternal in communion with God.

Notwithstanding the different emphases of these atonement "theories" (which can be seen as complementary rather than alternative), all churches assign atonement and reconciliation to the triune God. This is the heart of the Christian theology of atonement, and it also distinguishes it from most other religious accounts. In Christian theology, the human being can never work out salvation for oneself—nor can another human person; only God is able to.

In sum: the crux of Christian vision of salvation is the life, ministry, suffering, death, and resurrection of Jesus Christ. This is also the most radical and most foundational difference from Islam (and Judaism). No wonder a number of severe rebuttals and rejections have emerged from the Muslim side.

Muslim Rebuttals and Rejection of Christ's Salvific Work

As much as Jesus of Nazareth's significant role in both religions helps draw Christians and Muslims together around a common dialogue table, his death on the cross is a true scandal and cause of division. There is a sharp difference between Christianity and Islam in terms of both the source and the means of salvation: "The cross stands between Islam and Christianity. Dialogue cannot remove its scandal, and in due course a Muslim who might come to believe in Jesus has to face it."[1]

One of the reasons the suffering Messiah does not appeal to Muslims is that "paragons of success and vindication" such as Abraham, Noah, Moses, and David are much more congenial with the vision of God's manifest victory on earth. Simply put, "Islam refuses to accept this tragic image of [the] Passion. Not simply because it has no place for the dogma of the Redemption, but because the Passion would imply in its eyes that God had failed."[2] Understandably, attacks against the Christian teaching of the crucifixion have played a significant role in Muslim anti-Christian polemics and continue to do so, as illustrated in the widely influential pamphlet by the Indian–South African Ahmed Deedat, *Crucifixion or Cruci-fiction?*[3]

As already mentioned in chapter 4, this is the way the Qur'an narrates the event of the cross (which is also the only explicit reference to the crucifixion of Jesus), Q 4:157–58:

> And for their saying, "We slew the Messiah, Jesus son of Mary, the Messenger of God." And yet they did not slay him nor did they crucify him, but he was given the resemblance [or: "but a semblance was made to them"]. And those who disagree concerning him are surely in doubt regarding him. They do not have any knowledge of him, only the pursuit of conjecture; and they did not slay him for certain. Nay, God raised him up to Him [or: But Allah took him up unto Himself]. God is ever Mighty, Wise.[4]

While Muslim tradition does not speak with one voice about what really happened on the cross, it is safe to say that for most Muslims, if death on the cross even happened in the first place, it was not Jesus who died but rather a substitute ("semblance") in his stead. As to who this substitute might have been, the name of Simon of Cyrene is the standard answer but there are also others, including Judas of Iscariot. Jesus himself, instead of dying on the cross, was taken up to heaven by Allah, from whence he will return at the eschaton (more in chapter 10).

1. Bebawi, "Atonement and Mercy," 185.
2. Merad, "Christ According to the Qur'an," 14, quoted in Leirvik, *Images*, 4.
3. Deedat, *Crucifixion or Cruci-fiction?*
4. Alternative translations by Robinson, *Christ in Islam*, 106.

Christian apologetic has advanced two interrelated positions as a response to the standard Muslim denial of Jesus' death on the cross.[5] The first one is that the Qur'an is inconsistent. On the one hand, it seems to be affirming the death of Jesus (Q 19:33; 3:55[6]) and on the other hand, it is clearly denying it (Q 4:157). The second apologetic argument has advanced the thesis that, indeed, the Qur'an is not denying the crucifixion because the contested passage of 4:157–58 can be interpreted otherwise and because it is hard to deny the apparent affirmation of Jesus' death in other passages.

Be that as it may, even Muslim exegetes have widely debated the exact meaning of the passage "Allah took him up unto Himself" (v. 158). Similarly, the reference to "a semblance was made to them" in 4:157 (following Robinson) is difficult. Muslim theology agrees with Robinson's conclusion almost unanimously: "Despite differences of opinion about the details the commentators were agreed that 4:157 denies that Jesus was crucified. The most widespread view was that it implies that the Jews erroneously crucified Jesus' 'semblance' and not Jesus himself."[7]

These debates aside, what is clear and without dispute is that in standard Muslim understanding "'God was *not* in Christ reconciling the world to himself': he was with Jesus withdrawing him to heaven."[8] Sin is not atoned for through a substitutionary death in Islam, so Jesus' death on our behalf does not even make sense in the framework. Hence, Muslim and Christian accounts of reconciliation are even further from each other than Jewish from Christian accounts.

In sum: the whole of Muslim theology unanimously "denies the expiatory sacrifice of Christ on the Cross as a ransom for sinful humanity."[9] Nor would such a sacrificial, atoning death be needed. For, similarly to Judaism, Muslim theology lacks a doctrine of the fall and sinfulness after the Christian tradition.

5. This paragraph is based on Robinson, *Christ in Islam*, 108–110.

6. "And peace be upon me the day I was born, and the day I die, and the day I shall be raised alive!" (19:33); "When God said, 'O Jesus, I am gathering you, and raising you to Me, and I am cleansing you of those who disbelieved, and I am setting those who follow you above those who disbelieved until the Day of Resurrection. Then to Me shall be your return, and I will decide between you, as to what you were at variance about" (3:55).

7. Robinson, *Christ in Islam*, 140, at the end of the chapter-long detailed study of this expression in the Qur'an and commentary literature.

8. Cragg, *Jesus and the Muslim*, 167–68.

9. Ayoub, "Towards an Islamic Christology," 94.

What about the positive Muslim teaching about the way of "salvation"? On the way to detailing its main outline, let us attempt a brief detour with some observations from the Jewish tradition, which, as the foundation for Christian teaching about atonement, offers some useful comparative ground for Islam-Christian engagement as well.

A Detour: Redemption in Jewish Tradition

By now, it has become clear that Jewish and Muslim interpretations share more in common with each other than Christian views do with either one of them. Recall that instead of original sin, the Jewish (rabbinic) tradition speaks of two tendencies: good and evil. What matters is which of the two inclinations is the guiding force in life. Hence, the main term for repentance from evil is *teshuvah*, literally "turning" (to God).[10] While, as discussed previously, this is not to undermine the seriousness of sin and moral evil, nor is there any idea of original sin after Christian interpretation.

No wonder, then, that rather than "salvation," Jewish theology speaks typically of "redemption." The key idea of the term, which appears well over 100 times in the Old Testament, has to do with deliverance. Consider also how often the term "redeemer" (and "to redeem") appears in the most common Jewish daily prayer, the Amidah, including already in the opening paragraph, which extols Yahweh "who, in love, brings a redeemer to their children's children."[11] While not limited to national deliverance, the idea is present in most Jewish traditions even beyond Zionism. Similar to creation, which is the work of the past, present, and future, redemption also covers all tenses from the past to the future consummation.

What about faith and belief? According to Israel Abrahams, in the Jewish "Bible there are no articles of faith or dogmas in the Christian or Islamic sense of the terms." Rather than invitation to believe (in an intellectual sense), the biblical call is for faithfulness, which can be used of both God and the human person. The reason for the absence of catechism (in the Christian sense) is the emphasis on conduct and ethics. That is not to deny the presence of theological reflection and doctrines in

10. Kepnes, "Turn Us to You."

11. An English translation can be found at Chabad.org, "Translation of the Weekday Amidah."

later Judaism. Those came, however, largely because of apologetic need and external pressure. The Shema (Deut 6:4) is of course the basis and foundation of Jewish faith. Yet monotheism is more than a belief; it is the central thrust of Jewish (and Islamic) faith tradition.[12]

As discussed, even the Messiah is not the Savior in Christian sense of eternal life; rather, he is the deliverer who sets right the wrongs and helps redeem the promises of Yahweh to the fathers. Jews are still awaiting the Messiah; for Christians he has arrived.

Although the sacrificial system is part of the Jewish tradition, the Christian idea of vicarious atonement, on which the salvation of the world is based, is not part of Jewish theology because "the problem of sin had already been dealt with in the Torah."[13] Particularly in Talmudic traditions, "The sages know nothing of a miraculous redemption of the soul by external means. There is no failing in man, whether collectively or as an individual, which requires special divine intervention and which cannot be remedied, with the guidance of the Torah, by man himself."[14] Following the Torah and its commandments, as the chosen people, and thus testifying to God's unity and holiness, is the way of "salvation" in Judaism.[15]

Broadly speaking, notwithstanding debates and diversity in contemporary Jewish theology, this much can be said: "In modern Jewish thought redemption has been viewed as referring to the eventual triumph of good over evil, to the striving of individuals to self-fulfillment, to the achievement of social reforms, and also in terms of the reestablishment of a sovereign Jewish state."[16] This summative statement alone helps us see the substantial difference even between the mother faith of Israel and Christian theology of salvation. And when moving now to the youngest Abrahamic faith, the difference is being intensified.

Submission and Overcoming Ignorance in Islam

Recall that Islam's understanding of the human condition is closer to that of Judaism than to Christianity. Even more vehemently than the Jews, Muslims deny all notions of original sin and basically affirm the

12. Abrahams et al., "Belief," 291.
13. Kogan, *Opening the Covenant*, 116.
14. Leslie et al., "Redemption," 152.
15. Kogan, *Opening the Covenant*, 11–13.
16. Leslie et al., "Redemption," 154.

goodness of human nature. Needless to say, the Christian notion of the lostness of humanity does not resonate at all. The parallel to the idea of "lostness" is the ignorance of the right way and unwillingness to submit to Allah, acts that are conscious choices.

For these and related reasons having to do particularly with the rejection of all notions of Jesus' deity, Muslims do not envision redemption in the way Christian tradition does, namely, as a divine gift, and therefore there is absolutely no doctrine of atonement.[17] Nor does sacrifice play any salvific role at all. Muslim theology has a hard time intuiting why the justice and fairness of God would ever require a sacrifice and shedding of blood. Allah is of course sovereignly free to forgive (or not to forgive) apart from any such requirements, they surmise. And on the basis of Qur'anic teaching, it may be legitimate to infer that no one else can "pay" for the sins of others, not even Allah.[18]

This is not to deny the presence of grace and mercy in Islam. Even a cursory look at the Qur'an shows the prevalence of the idea of Allah as merciful. We have already established the gracious and merciful nature of God (see chapter 2). Recall that each and every sura (save sura 9) begins with extolling Allah's grace and mercy. Consider also this important sura: "Had it not been for the grace of Allah and His mercy unto you, not one of you would ever have grown pure" (Q 24:21, Marmaduke Pickthall trans.).

That mercy, however, does not translate in Islam into an idea of "justification by faith." Everything is about submitting to the will of Allah, particularly by observing the Five Pillars. Access to paradise will be granted as "a reward for what they used to do" (Q 56:24). Allah is a forgiving God and even a wayward person may seek forgiveness: "O My servants who have been prodigal against their own souls, do not despair of God's mercy. Truly God forgives all sins. Truly He is the Forgiving, the Merciful" (Q 39:53). But divine forgiveness is conditional on submission to Allah accompanied with good deeds and good character, as detailed in Q 33:35:

> Indeed the men who have submitted [to God] and the women who have submitted [to God], and the believing men and the believing women, and the obedient men and the obedient women, and the men who are truthful and the women who are truthful, and the patient men and the patient women, and the humble

17. Zebiri, *Muslims and Christians*, 216–17.

18. "Every soul earns only against itself; and no burdened soul shall bear the burden of another . . ." (Q 6:164).

> men and the humble women, and the charitable men and the charitable women, and the men who fast and the women who fast, and the men who guard their private parts and the women who guard their private parts, and the men who remember God often and the women who remember God often—for them God has prepared forgiveness and a great reward.

Where the mercy of Allah comes to the fore is in the completion beyond the balancing act of good and bad, as evidenced in the following statements:

- "Whoever brings a good deed, he shall have ten like it, and whoever brings an evil deed, he shall be recompensed only with the like of it, and they shall not be dealt with unjustly" (Q 6:160, Shakir trans.).
- "If you lend God a good loan, He will multiply it for you and He will forgive you, and God is Appreciative, Forbearing" (Q 64:17).

While one's efforts and good deeds certainly are required to gain access to paradise, God's mercy is also necessary as a surplus. It is in this respect that the numerous references to the merciful nature of Allah have to be interpreted. According to the Islamic tradition, this principle applied even to the Prophet himself.

To summarize, "salvation" in Islam means simply submission to Allah. But the fact that salvation ultimately depends on whether or not one wishes to submit does not mean that believing is thus marginalized. At least these six mandatory tenets of faith should be fully endorsed, namely the unity of God, divine predestination, angels, Qur'an, prophets, and the last day.[19] One cannot submit if one persists in ignorance of the revealed will of God.

Belief, however, is more than mere "head knowledge." It has to go hand in hand with repentance: "whereas those who repent and believe and act righteously—such shall enter Paradise and shall not be wronged in any way" (Q 19:60).[20] Belief is also to be accompanied with good deeds: "And those that believe, and perform righteous deeds, We shall admit them to Gardens . . ." (Q 4:57).[21]

19. For details, see Muhammad, *Compendium of Muslim Theology*, 3–15.

20. So also Q 3:16–17: "Those who say: 'O, Our Lord, we believe; so forgive us our sins, and guard us from the chastisement of the Fire, the patient, truthful, obedient, expenders, imploring God's pardon at daybreak.'"

21. The same is also stated in Q 4:122.

While submission to Allah is a personal matter, in Islam it is also integrally linked with the *ummah* (community) and confession of faith. In its widest sense, the "total submission of human will to the will of God" is expressed in three forms:

1. Through *islam*, which determines the institutionalized way of worshiping God.
2. Through *iman*, which is faith in God, his angels, his prophets, his books—all the revealed books of God—and the last day, that is, the day of resurrection.
3. Through *ahsan*, which refers to good actions, or righteous living, and which the Prophet interpreted as worshiping God "as though you see him, for if you do not see him he nonetheless sees you." So to be a true *muslim* (that is, to be in "submission" to God), whether you are a Christian, a Jew, a Hindu, a Buddhist, or whatever, is always to live in the presence of God.[22]

Indicative of the distinct nature of Islamic vision of "salvation" is the word which appears frequently in the Qur'an, *furqan* (Q 2:53, 185; 3:4; 8:29, 42; 21:48; 25:1). Its basic meaning is "distinction" or "criterion" (between right and wrong).[23] Distinctive also is another term, *falah,* which means "success." The main point is not only that success may happen both in this life and in the life to come but also that ultimately the human person is faced either with a positive outcome, success, or a negative one, failure.

While deliverance from sin does not have to be excluded from the Islamic vision of salvation, it is fair to say that deliverance from eternal punishment, often depicted as the "fire"[24] of hell, seems to be at the forefront.[25] Indeed, "'salvation' in the *Qur'an* is not the bestowal of a new creation, nor an act of power and victory over sin and death; rather, it is primarily an escape from judgment and entry into paradise."[26]

What about "assurance of salvation"? Although Qur'anic promises to those who believe and do good deeds seem assuring, there are also warnings throughout not to fall away: "Those who believe and *have not*

22. Ayoub, "Trinity Day Lectures," 8.

23. Esposito, ed., "Furqan, al-."

24. See, e.g., sura 2 in which it appears numerous times: 2:24, 39, 80–81, 119, 126, 167, 174–75, 201, 217, 221, 257, 266, 275.

25. Robson, "Aspects of the Qur'anic Doctrine," 205–6.

26. Greear, "Theosis and Muslim Evangelism," 130.

confounded their belief with evildoing, theirs is security; and they are rightly guided" (Q 6:82; my emphasis). Although one may lose salvation, every believer can also trust Allah's "guidance" (an almost technical term in the Qur'an referring to the divine help for believers such as in 6:157: "Now indeed a clear proof has come to you from your Lord, and a guidance and a mercy . . ."). Note that mercy is linked with guidance in this verse. Ultimately, Allah is absolutely sovereign in his dealings with humanity, and therefore the Christian (Calvinistic) idea of the "perseverance of the saints" according to which all elected necessarily keep their salvation whatsoever happens, is foreign to Islam.

As in other faith traditions, in Islam there are powerful mystical and even charismatic movements with beliefs and teachings marginal, at times even opposite, to the official doctrine briefly outlined here. The biggest and most well-known movement, known under the umbrella name Sufism, focuses on personal devotion and repentance. Sufi mysticism has an amazingly wide appeal among the ordinary faithful, probably influencing deeply more than half of all Muslims. In their spirituality the idea of union with God—theologically a most scandalous idea in light of normal Muslim teaching—comes to the forefront. As problematic as it appears to be in light of Muslim faith and theology, it seems to fill the hunger among the ordinary believers in Islam at large, a feature to be found in all living traditions!

Final Reflection: The Need for Continuing Careful and Patient Dialogue

To sum up briefly: Ignorance of the right path and unwillingness to submit to Allah are the main salvific needs in Islam. Redemption is not a divine gift but rather a result of right choice based on the revelation in the book. Unlike in Christian theology, in Islamic theology wrong choices cannot be atoned.

Undoubtedly, in many ways Judaism and Islam are closer to each other in terms of human diagnosis and its solution than they are to Christianity. In relation to both, the dividing issue is christological. With all the diversity of Christian views regarding the human condition and its solution, they all are christologically directed. Hence, a deep gulf separates Jewish and Muslim views from the view of Christ as the gate, source, and goal of salvation.

Furthermore, even though Jewish and Christian religions are Messianic, their Messianism is so different that it does not build a bridge with regard to salvation. For the mother faith, the Messiah is yet to appear, and when that happens, the Messiah is not the savior; Torah (and ultimately Yahweh, the giver of the law) is.

Islam's denial of the sinfulness of humanity—not *empirically*, as in denying that there is something wrong with us, but rather *theologically*, meaning that men and women will not be denied salvation due to some kind of innate sin—is the foundational obstacle for the Christian side. Regarding Jesus Christ, somewhat similarly to the figure of Messiah between Jewish and Christian teachings, he is as much a divider as the common denominator. The blunt and categorical denial of Jesus' atoning death (regardless of historical nuances) blocks the way of salvation by faith through grace to the Muslim, according to the basic Christian vision.

This fairly rigid summative categorization and comparison is not meant to stall dialogue! Had it been done apart from a careful comparative investigation into authoritative teachings of each tradition, that might have been the implication. This stark picture of the differences among these three cousin faiths is rather meant to demonstrate the need for careful, painstaking, and patient comparative dialogue. As a way of encouragement, recall that resources for this work are immense between Judaism, Islam, and Christianity: partially shared scriptural tradition, monotheism, and a number of shared doctrines, including creation, eschatology, and others.

9

Any Divine Spirit(s) in Islam?

Of all Christian doctrines and beliefs, only a few are as unknown to most Christians than the doctrine of the Holy Spirit, a.k.a. pneumatology (from the Greek term *pneuma*, "spirit" or "wind"). While it makes much more sense to speak about Father and Son to whom there exist concrete counterparts in our life, this is much less so with the Spirit and spirits. Particularly in our secular and science-driven times, all talk about the Spirit/spirits may easily turn into "ghost"-like discourse. And of course, in the older English translations, the term "Holy Ghost" was used for the third member of the Trinity!

On the other hand, religions seem to be talking quite a lot about all kinds of spiritual phenomena, spiritual beings, and spiritual experiences. As the Indian Christian theologian Joseph Pathrapankal states, the Spirit is "the foundational reality which makes possible for the humans to exercise their religious sense and elevate their self to the realm of the divine."[1] No wonder, then, that part of the cosmic orientation of all traditional and most contemporary cultures outside the West has to do with the deep and wide sense of spirits and spiritualities. Even beyond religions, human history has always taken for granted that beyond the visible, physical causes of events there are spirits, even divine spirits, in fact the spirit world. Although the Enlightenment challenged this state of affairs with its turn to physical, materialist explanations, particularly among the educated elites in the Global North, the reality of the spirit world is still taken

1. Pathrapankal, "Editorial," 299.

for granted and embraced particularly in the Global South—and in many quarters of the North as well. Hence, notwithstanding the complexity and strangeness of the topic, no authentically comparative encounter should dismiss spirit-talk.

But what about Islam's take on the Spirit/spirit(s)? Does it really have a "pneumatology" of its own or conceptions of spiritual beings and phenomena? Does it make sense to compare notes with Christian theology? Yes, it does—indeed, very much so. And that alone both justifies and necessitates this brief discussion.

What Is Christian Pneumatology All About?

In Christian theology, the Holy Spirit is both a person, the third person of the Trinity, and divine spirit and energy, enlightening, creating, and sustaining all life, even the whole cosmos. This divine energy was an integral part of the original creation as well, the principle of life and liveliness. The same Holy Spirit as a special salvific gift also breathes new life to those who are reborn into Christian faith, sanctifying, guiding, and empowering.

In Christian theology, the third member of the Trinity, the Holy Spirit, is fully divine along with the other two Trinitarian members, a conviction established in the early centuries of the faith. Not surprisingly, similarly to the doctrine of the Trinity and Christology, it took a few centuries for the then worldwide Christian community to come to a stated creedal understanding of the Spirit. In fact, the so-called third article of faith (following the first on the Father and second on the Son) took the longest time to be formulated and finalized. A major challenge was to lift up, so to speak, the Spirit to the same level of deity as the Father and Son.

According to biblical testimonies, the Holy Spirit functions everywhere in the world and in Christian faith, from serving as the principle of life giving birth and sustaining living beings and creation, to inspiring Scripture and enlivening its reading in the Christian community, to helping distinguish between God-sent spirits and their opponents, and so forth. That said, the Holy Spirit is looked upon particularly as the agent who brings to men and women the salvific gifts acquired by the Son in his incarnation, suffering, death, and resurrection. Throughout history, and more recently in the rapidly growing Pentecostal/charismatic movement, the Spirit's empowering charisms have also been highlighted, including healing and prophecy.

Under and subservient to the Holy Spirit (and more widely, the triune God), Christian tradition, based on the biblical teaching, knows spiritual powers and energies, named angels and demons. Teaching on these spiritual powers is less fully developed than the doctrine of the Holy Spirit (proper), and they are typically conceived of as created beings who possess some real power (and often also, their own will). As to the origin of demons and evil powers, mythical stories allegedly hinted at in the biblical canon are often mentioned, though no clear canonical opinion exists.

Now to the task of profiling a typical Islamic pneumatology.

Spirit in the Qur'an

To no reader's surprise, the Muslim teaching about the Spirit is deeply indebted to older Abrahamic traditions. The basic term *ruh* is, of course, a Hebrew cognate with shared meanings of breath, wind, and air. Briefly defined, it can be stated that "The spirit is a creation of God that does not have a material, temporal, or gradual origination. It is a means of spiritual support that is also not material, temporal or gradual."[2]

In the Qur'an there are about twenty references to *ruh*. A useful way to study the Islamic understanding is to divide these references under four categories, named as "sense-groups."[3] Looking at and analyzing these various sense-groups helps profile and expand pneumatology in Islam.

The first sense-group relates to the sayings about the angels and the spirit: "The angels and the Spirit descend in it by the leave of their Lord with every command" (Q 97:4). The context of the passage relates to the "Night of Power" when the Word of God was communicated via the angel Gabriel to the Prophet. This in itself is an important connection with the Christian tradition, in which the Word of God is also closely related to the Spirit of God. You may also recall that in New Testament (Heb 1:14) the term designating angels is ministering "spirits." The nature of the Spirit in this and related verses is between the divine energy and personhood, to use the Christian language; perhaps the word "semi-personified" might be proper.

2. Raja, "Spirit and the Word," para. 1.

3. O'Shaughnessy, *Development of the Meaning of Spirit in the Koran*, 67–68.

The second sense-group is about the sharing of Allah's spirit with humans. Here the Qur'an makes a definite shift from a (semi-)personal agent to an impersonal breath, as in Genesis 2:7: "then the LORD God formed man of dust from the ground, and breathed into his nostrils the breath of life; and man became a living being." In Islam, this breathing relates only to two persons:

- Adam when Allah "proportioned him and breathed of My Spirit in him" (Q 15:29; the same repeated in 32:9 and 38:72); and
- Jesus, including the virginal conception by Mary "whereupon We sent to her Our Spirit, and he assumed before her the likeness of a well-proportioned human" (Q 19:17).[4] Even more astonishing is the widely debated passage both among the Muslim and Christian interpreters in which Jesus is named a S/spirit from Allah, alongside the work of the Spirit in virginal conception: "the Messiah, Jesus the son of Mary, was only the Messenger of God, and His Word which He cast to Mary, and a spirit from Him (Q 4:171).

Let us pause here and inquire into the meaning of this last, mysterious passage: What, indeed, is the meaning of the Qur'anic saying that Jesus is a spirit from Allah? We have to hasten to mention that while for the Christian this kind of saying clearly resonates with the idea of the deity of Jesus, there is nothing of that sort in Islam. Not even the very Christian-like description of Jesus, the Messiah, as the "Word" of God, establishes any kind of divine nature or status in Islam. Furthermore, as previously discussed, the reference to Jesus as Messiah, as unique as it is in Islamic tradition, is to be interpreted as a high-level messenger, no more. This interpretation is easily confirmed by the very same verse we are considering (Q 4:171):

> O People of the Scripture, do not go to extremes, in your religion and do not say about God except the truth: the Messiah, Jesus the son of Mary, was only the Messenger of God, and His Word which He cast to Mary, and a spirit from Him. So believe in God and His messengers, and do not say, "Three." Refrain, it

4. See also these important verses: "And the one who guarded her virginity, so We breathed into her of Our spirit. And We made her and her son a sign for all the worlds" (Q 21:91); "And Mary daughter of 'Imrān, who preserved [the chastity of] her womb, so We breathed into it of Our Spirit, and she confirmed the words of her Lord and His Scriptures, and she was of the obedient" (Q 66:12).

> is better for you. Verily, God is but One God. Glory be to Him, that He should have a son!

In sum: the main point of the sayings belonging under the grouping two parallel quite closely the Christian understanding of the Spirit as the divine energy but have no connotations of deity either with regard to the Spirit or Jesus.

The third sense-group of *ruh* sayings in the Qur'an is the least understood:

- "And they will question you concerning the Spirit. Say: 'The Spirit is of the command [*amr*] of my Lord. And of knowledge you have not been given except a little'" (Q 17:85).
- "He sends down the angels with the Spirit of His command [*amr*] to whomever He will of His servants" (Q 16:2).

The exact meaning of *amr* is disputed: Is it "command" or "affair" or something else? At the moment, even Muslim experts do not speak with one voice; so, it is of course best for us to leave open this mysterious expression (which also appears elsewhere, as in Q 40:15).

The final sense-group relates to the important theme of the "Holy Spirit," the "Spirit of Holiness": "Say: 'The Holy Spirit has revealed it from your Lord with truth to confirm [the faith of] those who believe, and as guidance and good tidings for those who have submitted [to God]'" (Q 16:102). Importantly, there are three verses in which the Holy Spirit is linked with Jesus in terms of Allah "strengthening" or "confirming" him: "And We gave Moses the Scripture, and after him We sent successive messengers, and We gave Jesus son of Mary the clear proofs, and We confirmed him with the Holy Spirit . . ." (Q 2:87; the same repeated in verse 253). Quite astonishing is the verse that mentions that "when I strengthened you [Jesus] with the Holy Spirit to speak to people in the cradle and in maturity . . ." (Q 5:110).

Furthermore, it is noteworthy that not only Jesus but also some other faithful are also strengthened with a spirit from Allah (Q 58:22):

> [For] those He has inscribed faith upon their hearts and reinforced them with a spirit from Him, and He will admit them into gardens underneath which rivers flow, wherein they will abide, God being pleased with them, and they being pleased with Him. Those [they] are God's confederates. Assuredly it is God's confederates who are the successful.

In sum: this brief consideration of the teaching of the Qur'an about the Spirit/spirit has many meanings and contexts, another similarity with the Christian pneumatology notwithstanding their marked difference in identifying who the S/spirit is. Whereas for Christians the Spirit is not only divine but also God, in Islam the contours of who or what the S/spirit is are left open and elusive. The only sure thing that can be said is that even the Holy Spirit (Spirit of Holiness) is definitely neither divine nor deity.

Mystical and Charismatic Experiences of the Spirit

Again, with all the theological differences, yet another similarity between the two traditions' pneumatologies is that the Spirit is not only a matter of doctrinal debates and analyses but rather an energy, power to be experienced and celebrated. Unbeknownst to many Christians only thinly familiar with global Islam, grassroots-level enthusiasm of the spiritual experience, similar to that found in other faiths, is manifest everywhere in folk Islam. The charismatic-mystical life and experiences are particularly common among various movements at the grassroots level, and certainly in Sufi Islam, which by definition pays a lot more attention to spiritual experiences.

As mentioned, the mystically and charismatically oriented Sufi spirituality—not limited to the fairly small number of Sufi movements per se—is present among most Muslim traditions and communities. The rapid and steady growth of Sufism and related spiritualist movements is explained at least partly by the full embrace of the spiritual experience and manifestations.

No wonder that throughout the years "power encounter" and miraculous acts have been enthusiastically acknowledged and claimed to lie behind many conversions. A particularly important role is played by mystical dreams and visions behind growing interest in the Christian message and conversion from Islam.

As with many such renewal movements and experiences, at times the contours of doctrinal purity are tested. We noticed the same above with the question of what constitutes "salvation" and spiritual pursuit in Sufi-type of spirituality. A highly illustrative example is Sufism's virtual identification of the Spirit of Holiness/Holy Spirit with God himself, an idea clearly flirting with the gravest sin of *shirk*. Another one, even more dramatic, is the experience of the famous ninth-century Sufi mystic Husayn ibn Mansur Al-Hallajah. In keeping with his spirituality's focus on love and spiritual unity, it was said of him that the mystic "was so full of the Holy Spirit that he could no longer distinguish himself from God," an abomination to the establishment, leading to his crucifixion in 922.[5]

An Interesting Case Study: Is Muhammad the Johannine "Comforter"?

As repeatedly mentioned, the fascination and challenge of Muslim-Christian exchange is the deep and wide dependence of Islam on Christian (and, of course, Jewish) sources and teachings. With all the dramatic differences in interpretation, the anchoring of Islamic doctrine in the two earlier traditions also raises questions that are surprising and even astonishing. One of the classical ones stands at the heart of pneumatology. It has to do with whether Muhammad, the Prophet himself, might be what the Gospel of John in chapters 14 and 16 names (in Greek) the *Parakletos*, the Advocate, the Comforter, in other words, the Holy Spirit! How on earth, one may ask, has this kind of odd question even emerged? Let us take a closer look.

The crux of the issue is simply this: While not universally held among the Muslims, there is a long and wide tradition of identifying the Paraclete with Muhammad. Particularly in folk Islam, that is more or less a dogmatic opinion. The issue goes back to the interpretation of Qur'an 61:6 and its connection to John 15:26–27 and 16:7:

> And when Jesus son of Mary said, "O Children of Israel I am indeed God's messenger to you, confirming what is before me of the Torah and bringing good tidings of a messenger who will come after me, whose name is Ahmad." Yet when he brought them, they said, "This is manifest sorcery!" (Q 61:6).

> "Nevertheless I tell you the truth: it is to your advantage that I go away, for if I do not go away, the Counselor [*parakletos*] will not come to you; but if I go, I will send him to you" (John 16:7).

The *parakletos* ("Counselor") of John 16:7 is equated with "Ahmad" of Qur'an 61:6 (in many English renderings, the "Praised One"). In Islamic tradition, a version of Muhammad's name is Ahmad. There

5. Kritzeck, "Holy Spirit in Islam," 110.

are, however, a number of problems with this identification, the most obvious one being that there is absolutely no textual evidence for it in Greek manuscripts of the New Testament. Furthermore, it is doubtful that Muhammad himself would have endorsed this interpretation. There are also several other reasons that speak against this identification, not least the fact that the Christian doctrine of the Spirit's (the Comforter's) deity is categorically denied in Islam.

How, then, could Muhammad be a counterpart to God, a totally impossible conception in Islam? The late and venerated Islamic expert and Christian bishop Kenneth Cragg summarizes it well concerning the Muslim allegation of Qur'an 61:1 interpretation arguing for the identity of the two:

> What is certainly clear is that it cannot be related to the sayings of Jesus in the Gospels about the Paraclete. Those sayings in no way relate to a purely prophetic spokesman whose coming, six centuries after, would in no sense be relevant to Jesus' disciples in their immediate first-century situation. His promise was to them and to their posterity in unbroken sequence. It did not, in its Gospel context, relate to a generation fifteen generations on, and after a silent hiatus of non-fulfilment.[6]

Having now sketched an outline of the Muslim conception of the Spirit of Allah and its similarity with and difference from Christian pneumatology at large, it is time to focus on the question of spirits, spiritual beings, and spiritual manifestations. As with so many other topics, it is useful first to describe briefly the Christian vision and then give major part to the Islamic in an attempt to continue comparison of notes and learning from each other.

Angels, Demons, and Spiritual Powers in Christian Tradition

If the Divine Spirit is omnipresent in God's creation, then even those realities that biblical and Christian terminology identifies as "powers," angels, and demons are related to pneumatology. In fact, both the Bible and early theology understood these spiritual realities as *realities* rather than merely superstitious fantasies. At the same time, notwithstanding occasional overenthusiasm, the early church father Origen reminded us: "Regarding the devil and his angels, and the opposing influences,

6. Cragg, *Jesus and the Muslim*, 266.

the teaching of the Church has laid down that these beings exist indeed; but what they are, or how they exist, it has not explained with sufficient clearness."[7]

Biblical testimonies to angels and spiritual powers abound—with the curious exception of the creation narratives of Genesis 1–2. Particularly significant for our purposes is the naming of heavenly, angelic forces as "spirits" (Greek *pneumata*) (Heb 1:14, 12:9; Rev 1:4; etc.). It is important to keep in mind that even spiritual beings are created beings; only God is uncreated.

The New Testament teaches that spiritual beings are not only created in Christ (Col 1:16) but also subjected under his lordship (2:15). By subordinating the role of both good and evil angels and powers to God, the Bible avoids dualism, that is, there would be two more or less equally powerful ultimate realities, God and God's opponent. Even the role of Satan, which evolved gradually over the course of history, is that of a subordinate, and in some cases even of a servant of God, as in the beginning of the book of Job.

Angels are mentioned in numerous biblical passages. Their appearance takes place typically in important revelatory and salvific and at times judgmental events and processes. The angels' main role is to act as God's messengers and aides. The most curious among these beings is the "Angel of the Lord" (for example in Gen 16:7–13), a semi-divine figure widely understood by Christians as a prototype of the pre-existent Christ.

The appearance of demons, which are always evil spiritual beings, is depicted here and there in the Old Testament, including in accounts of cosmic conflict and chaos (Job 3:8, 38:8–11; Ps 29:3–4, 89:9–10; Isa 51:9–11). In the first three Gospels, Jesus' encounters with evil spirits are quite frequent and, alongside healing, casting out, and silencing the demonic, are an important sign of the kingdom of God.

Notwithstanding this plethora of references, the Bible curiously provides preciously few details about the angels and spiritual forces, including their emergence. Nor does the Bible really teach us what prompted the distinction between good and bad angels, although it clearly affirms the existence of evil angels (Matt 25:41; 2 Pet 2:4; Jude 1:6; Rev 12:9). The Christian tradition's assumption about the angelic fall (including of Satan) is based on only a couple of obscure passages (Isa 14:12–14; Ezek 28:12–19), and is merely that—an *assumption*.

7. Origen, *First Principles*, *ANF* 4:240.

Nor does the biblical witness give us a definitive answer about whether angels, good and evil, are personal in nature, though it often treats them in a way that suggests a nonpersonal nature: seven spirits or lampstands, torches, stars, and so forth (Rev 1:4–20). Importantly, the New Testament also uses terms such as "principalities," "powers," and "thrones" (Rom 8:38–39; 1 Cor 15:24; Eph 1:21; 1 Pet 3:22). Yet at times the text suggests these entities' personal nature, for example by speaking of their intelligence and will (1 Kgs 22:19–21; Dan 10:5–21; Matt 4:3–11; Mark 5:6–13). Be that as it may, both the biblical and the historical-theological teaching and imagination of the church envisions a great variety of spiritual powers and "beings."

Islam's Fascination with Spiritual Beings and Phenomena

Of the three Abrahamic faiths, it is in Islam that angels and spiritual beings play the most significant role, whether in scriptural tradition or in folk piety. As discussed, belief in angels is one of Islam's key tenets, and their denial is regarded as a rejection of the Word of God. Their importance is also highlighted in that, unlike in Jewish-Christian tradition, there is a well-known scriptural teaching about angels' creation prior to that of humans and about Allah's consultation with them before creating humans (Q 38:71–72[8]).

Somewhat similarly to the Old Testament, the Qur'an provides various kinds of artistic portraits of angels such as their having hands and two, three, or four wings (Q 6:93; 35:1[9]) and speaks of their ministering in various kinds of tasks of service and messaging, including intercession (Q 53:26[10]). A further similarity is an allusion to the hierarchy of angels, Gabriel being the most prominent, and Michael second. The most important angelic task is that of Gabriel as the messenger from whom Muhammad received the divine revelation. No wonder that highly sophisticated

8. "When your Lord said to the angels, 'Indeed I am about to create a human being out of clay. So when I have proportioned him, and breathed in him My spirit, then fall down in prostration before him!'"

9. If you could only see when the evildoers are in the agonies of death and the angels extend their hands . . ." (Q 6:93); "Praise be to God Originator of the heavens and the earth, Appointer of the angels as messengers, having wings in [sets of] two or three or four" (Q 35:1).

10. "And how many an angel there is in the heavens whose intercession cannot avail in any way except after God gives permission for whomever He wills, and He is satisfied" (Q 53:26).

angelologies were constructed by leading Islamic philosophers and theologians—not unlike those created by Christian theologians particularly during the medieval times.

A special class of heavenly beings, the *jinn*—hugely important in folk Islam—are mentioned often in the Qur'an. They are made of fire (as opposed to humans, who are made of clay). They are endowed with freedom of the will, and there is ambiguity about whether they are evil or good; mostly they are taken as evil. Jinns are believed to interact in various ways with humanity. In folk religion, they are frequently invoked for magical and miraculous purposes. Spiritual healers often address the jinn as part of their rituals.[11]

The counterpart to the Jewish-Christian archenemy of Satan is named in Islam as *Iblis*. When at the creation of the humanity, all angels were invited by God to prostrate themselves before Adam, Satan (named Iblis), who then promised to take Adam and Eve to the tree of immortality and knowledge, declined. While these details from the Qur'an's fall narrative are not to be found in the Bible, the basic idea of the emergence and nature of Satan is familiar:

> Satan was a favorite angel of God and was of great consequence in the order of the heavenly host until he disobeyed God's order and was expelled from paradise, incurring eternal damnation. Thus, Satan became the embodiment of everything evil, acquiring all the attributes that are incompatible with God. We note here that Satan's name indicates his essence, which is "*iblas*"—that is, total despair of God's mercy and of return to paradise (this according to traditional Muslim interpretations of the meaning of *iblas*).[12]

In sum: the spirit-world, including good and evil spiritual beings, spiritual manifestations, and spirit-experiences are alive and well in global Islam, not only in mystical movements such as Sufism but also both at the grassroots level and in teachings and sermons.

11. Newby, "Angels" and "Jinn."

12. Al-Azm, *Islam*, 132.

10

Is There a "Church" for Muslims?

Orientation: No Solitary Religion!

An integral part of living and ancient faith traditions is that the person never believes and practices his or her own religion alone. As personal as the commitment to one's faith might be, it is never without a group of like-minded joining the same commitment—even if, as it often happens, splits and divisions have begun to happen from early on. In fact, it seems like "it is part of the belief-structure of most religions that there should be a particular society which protects and sustains their basic values and beliefs, within which one may pursue the ideal human goal, as defined within the society."[1] That observation alone would justify the comparison of notes between Islam and Christianity, currently the two world's largest religions with the combined followership of almost two-thirds of the world's total population.

But to say that virtually all religions have a community to support faith and spirituality is not to say that therefore the meaning and significance of the community is identical across the religious spectrum. Far from it. For the purposes of our comparison between the visions of community in Islam and Christianity, it is highly useful to outline briefly these widely differing conceptions of the role of the community among religions. Let's do it with a broad brush in order to bring home the main point. Comparison is best done by considering the Abrahamic traditions on one side and

1. Ward, *Religion and Community*, 1.

the Asiatic faiths the other side (represented by Hinduism and Buddhism). That brief comparison brings to light notable differences.

First, whereas the Abrahamic traditions are integrally communal, neither of the Asiatic faiths engaged here is, notwithstanding the presence of the community at the center of their spiritual life. This means that for the faithful Buddhist or Hindu the main point of the spiritual quest and pursuit is one's own enlightenment or release. Accordingly, ultimately the Asiatic faiths' visions of "salvation" focuses on one's own self rather than on the whole of humanity or on the reconciliation of the cosmos, as is the case in Jewish-Christian tradition and, to a lesser extent, in Islam.

Second, whereas for Abrahamic traditions the religious community is rooted in God and divine election, in Asiatic faiths that is not the case. The religious community emerges around the founder and his legacy as in Buddhism, or as a loosely connected network of numerous, truly numerous, local communities, as in Hinduism gathering together people in search of each one's final release. Even when a Hindu community typically worships one of the numerous local deities, the community itself is not rooted in the god.

Third, whereas the Asiatic faiths seek to renounce the world in pursuit of final release, the Christian faith seeks both to renounce "the world" and to penetrate it with the gospel for the sake of God's kingdom and, in Islam, with its call for submission for the whole world.

Now, with this bigger picture about the role of the community among religions in mind, let us first outline briefly the Christian vision of the church to prepare us for profiling the Islamic community, *ummah*, for the sake of comparison. The rest of the chapter takes up a few mutually significant subtopics relevant to this discussion, including conversion and mission.

The Emergence and Vision of the Religious Community in Christianity

As established, community, the church, is absolutely important to Christian faith. Indeed, there are no solitary Christians if that means that one can become Christian and practice faith without any reference to the community which over millennia has carried the gospel message, the Bible, spiritual life, sacraments, and all other such necessary elements.

In light of the high importance of the church to Christian faith, it is no wonder that ecclesiology, the doctrine of the church, encompasses a wide array of interrelated topics, including

- the nature of the Christian community,
- the mission, ministry, and service to the world,
- the sacraments and liturgical life,
- the quest for the unity of the church in light of rampant divisions, and
- the relation to other faith traditions—and to the secular people.

As with all Christian doctrines, Jesus Christ plays a central role in ecclesiology—much more so than the Prophet in Islam. This means that Jesus Christ is both the founder of the church and its foundation! The newly born originally Jewish sect that at first worshipped in the Jewish synagogues developed into a separate community, the church, sometime after the resurrection of Christ from the dead and the ensuing pouring out of the Spirit of God on the day of Pentecost. In fact, Pentecost can be rightly named as the birthday of the church, at the end of the events stemming from the coming, ministry, suffering, death, and ascension of Jesus the Christ.

This means that, differently from Buddhism whose community, *sangha*, developed out of the band of earliest followers of the Gautama Buddha after his enlightenment, the church is more than just the sequel to the originally twelve-member band of disciples following Jesus of Nazareth during his earthly ministry. The church is also different from the Islamic *ummah*, which was born out of the coming together of a few family members and other earliest followers of the teaching of the Prophet Muhammad after his reception of revelation. Since neither Gautama nor Muhammad is in any way a Savior but rather the grand example to follow and the source of teaching, neither of the communities they helped found can be said to have their "foundation" in them.

To repeat: that the Christ is the foundation of the church is to say that on top of Jesus' teachings, healings, exorcisms, and the rest of the ministry, it is particularly his atoning death and his victorious resurrection that ushered in the Pentecostal power from on high to make the disciples' band the Christian church. Not for nothing, then, the church is called in New Testament the "body" of Christ, himself being the "head."

That is the metaphor of the closest possible union between the two. No wonder the word *church* has as its etymological root the Greek term *Kyriakos*, "belonging to the Lord." All this is something that would not make any sense with the *sangha* or *ummah*.

Alongside the body metaphor, among the numerous various images and symbols of the Christian community in the New Testament, the following two have become the most significant: the "people" of God links the church with Israel as the first people of God, and the "temple" of the Spirit speaks of the dual role of the Holy Spirit as the foundation of the church, reminding us of the Trinitarian basis of the church!

The church born on the day of the Pentecost was tasked by its Lord to continue the mission of the kingdom of God, the ushering in of the righteous rule of his Father, to be consummated in his second coming at the end of the ages. Catapulted into worldwide mission of proclamation, healing ministry, and service, this community has grown to be the largest in the history of religions, now encompassing about one-third of the world's population in all its diversity and plurality.

Following the example of the first Christian church, the church of the book of Acts, the Christian community has studied and listened to the Scripture; prayed and worshipped; practiced sacraments, particularly water baptism and the Eucharist (the two universal rites present in all communities); and cultivated communion (fellowship). Tightly linked with this "inner" life of the community, the church has also been involved in diverse ministries, including preaching, healing, exorcism, as well as service to the poor and other disadvantaged persons. This mission includes both local and global dimensions, as Christianity, alongside Islam and early Buddhism in particular, is a deeply missional faith, unlike Judaism and Hinduism.

While all Christian communities make a distinction (though not a separation) between the clergy and the laity, leadership patterns and practices as well as theologies of ordination (that is, setting apart for a professional, usually theologically trained, ministerial leadership) vary from one denomination to another. Historically the oldest way of organizing ministry is probably the three-tiered bishop, priest, and deacon/deaconess model. Alongside this pattern practiced in older churches (Orthodox, Roman Catholic) and the Anglican Church, there are two-tiered models, consisting of pastor and deacons, or something similar.

The worship and liturgical life of the church has never been uniform; yet, common elements can be found in weekly or other regular gatherings. They include reading the Scriptures, homily, prayers, singing, and sacraments. While the majority of churches expect the leader of the worship and liturgical gathering to be an ordained minister, particularly when it comes to administering the Eucharist, a growing number of churches may or may not have that rule.

Beginning from the early centuries, the one church of Christ has undergone divisions and splits. The most well-known dividing moments have been the 1054 split between what are now the Eastern (Orthodox) Church and the Western church (Roman Catholic, Anglican, Protestant, free churches, and independent communities). At the time of the sixteenth-century Reformation, the Western church further divided into two main families, Roman Catholics on one side and Anglicans and all Protestants on the other side. In the Protestant family of churches, originally Lutherans, Reformed, and Anglicans, the so-called free churches, beginning from the Anabaptists and Baptists, separated themselves. Thereafter, constant splits and divisions have continued and still continue to some extent.

The Rise of the Islamic Community

As stated, Islam as a religion shares with Judaism and Christianity a deep communal orientation. The term for the community, *ummah*, appears in the Qur'an more than sixty times, with diverse and varying meanings. Of course, it typically refers to the Muslim community itself, as in the following passages:

- "Our Lord! And make us submissive to You and, of our seed, a community submissive to You; and show us our holy rites, and relent to us. Surely You are the Relenting, the Merciful" (Q 2:128).
- "Thus, We appointed you a midmost community that you might be witnesses to the people; and that the Messenger might be a witness to you . . ." (Q 2:143).
- "You are the best community brought forth to men, enjoining decency, and forbidding indecency, and believing in God" (Q 3:110).

The term may also occasionally relate more widely to the "people of the Book," including the Jews as in Q 16:120: "Truly Abraham was a community, obedient to God," and even the Christians, as in Q 21:92: "Truly this is your community, one community, and I am your Lord, so worship

Me" (speaking of Mary and Jesus). This incipient universal vision of early Islam is evident in Q 10:19: "Mankind was but one community; then they differed," obviously implying that in the beginning there might have been just one *ummah* comprising also Jews and Christians.

Things, however, began to change over the course of the early history of Islam during the Prophet's lifetime. Beginning as more or less inclusive of Muslims, Jews, and Christians, based on belief in one God, it moved toward a narrower view limited basically to the followers of the Prophet. A definite limiting took place after his death, when *ummah* (with some occasional exceptions) included only the Muslims.

Not surprisingly, the idea of the superiority of this community began also to be established quite early, as illustrated in Q 3:110 cited above describing the *ummah* as "the best community" both in terms of belief and morality. As an interesting observation, consider in this light the following well-known, widely disputed passage: "Thus, We appointed you a midmost community that you might be witnesses to the people" (Q 2:143). What, indeed, does the term "midmost" (or "middle nation" or something similar in some other renderings) really mean—the best or the good example or something else?

The Early Split of the *Ummah*: Sunnis and Shi'ites

Whereas all living faiths have experienced severe and continuing internal divisions, with Islam it happened early and established stark borderlines between two major traditions. As briefly recounted in chapter 1, this major division, which gave rise to the major divide between Sunnis and Shi'ites, arose over the issue of the Prophet's successor after his death (in 632). Abu Bakr, the father of the Prophet's beloved wife Aisha, was made the first leader by the majority, but that did not settle the matter, as the minority of the community preferred Ali, the husband of Muhammad's daughter Fatima, as their leader. Both theological and political issues were involved.

Whereas for the majority the leadership choice after the passing of the Prophet belonged to the *ummah* at large, for the rest it was a divine choice falling on Ali—with the ambiguous claim that he had divine endorsement as well as that of the Prophet. The majority wanted to stay in the line of Mecca's dominant tribe, the Prophet's own tribe, Quraysh; whereas a minority received support from Medina. Full separation of the *ummah*, however, did not come about until after the brief leadership of Umar I and the longer office of the caliph Uthman, whose assassination in 656 brought Ali to power for half a decade, a period of virtual civil war. In the end, the community's separation was final, between the majority Sunnis (currently over 80 percent) and a minority of Shi'ites who followed Ali's legacy. Both sides continued splitting internally, leading to the kind of complex denominationalism characteristic of most religions.

Numerous historical, political, and related debates aside—which are best left to expert historians—let us only highlight this obvious observation: It is amazing and confusing to the outsider to the global Muslim community that, despite how much they share in tradition and doctrine, their mutual relationships are so antagonistic and condemnatory. Both parties share the same Qur'an, the same prophethood, and the Five Pillars, including prayers, fasting, and other rituals (albeit somewhat differently nuanced and practiced). Yet it seems that any kind of global ecumenical reconciliation is not on the horizon—although the Qur'an mandates work for unity. "And hold fast to God's bond, together, and do not scatter . . ." (Q 3:103–5). That said, it is worth repeating that whereas the Sunnis, the vast majority of the global Islam, represent "mainstream" Islam (and have their views taken routinely as *the* Muslim opinions, including in this primer), the minority Shi'ites also endorse basically all the same beliefs and practices. Over the course of history, as it often happens among religions, ethnic, nationalist, cultural, and political differences have intensified the internal division of the global *ummah*—to the point that it is not uncommon to encounter mutual condemnations to hell among main factions of this world religion.

What is distinctive about Shi'ites is a shared belief in the divinely ordered status of Ali as the successor to the Prophet—although, as is well-known, the Qur'an does not rule on the issue. The Twelvers, by far the largest and most important Shi'ite denomination, have developed a highly sophisticated genetic line of succession from Ali through his two sons (Hasan and Husayn) all the way to the Twelfth one. Its most distinctive claim has to do with the last imam (after Hasan ibn Ali al-Askari of the ninth century), titled Muhammad b. Hasan, who allegedly went into "occultation" (that is, concealment) and whose return is awaited. In this interpretation, all imams possess inerrancy in order to be able to prevent the community from being led astray. That said, there are a number of fiercely debated issues among the three main Shi'ite traditions (the Twelvers, the Ishmaelites, and the Zaydis, the first two sharing much more in common concerning the imamate) about the line of succession and related issues.

Be that as it may, similarly to all religious communities, the Islamic *ummah* has rites and rituals to follow. Let us move to consider them and keep in mind the comparative task at hand.

Spiritual Life and Worship

Recall that the crux of Muslim faith is to honor *tawhid*, the absolute unity and oneness of God, and relatedly, to submit to Allah in obedience and gratitude, including willing service. This forms the basis not only for Muslim life at large but also for the whole of spiritual life with devotion, prayer, and worship. Together these constitute the "Five Pillars"—confession, ritual prayer, fasting, pilgrimage, and alms—routinely preceded by the important rites of purification, both physical and spiritual.

The ritual prayer is the most visible form of piety. Muslims ought to pray five times a day at designated times, regardless of their location. Prayer is preceded by ablution and employs a prescribed form and content. Prayer is also the main activity in the mosque. Nowadays, the Friday-afternoon gathering there includes a sermon. Holy Scripture is highly honored and venerated. Since there is no clergy and no theologically trained priesthood, any male is in principle qualified to lead. He is usually chosen from among those most deeply knowledgeable in the Scripture and the tradition.

While distinctive, it is easy to see many similarities with Christian spirituality, which also includes the elements of prayer, fasting, alms, pilgrimage, and confession of faith. The difference is that apart from prayer, worship gatherings including the study of Scripture and sermon, none of the other five binding elements (to Muslims) are mandatory for most Christian communities. Some Christians fast, others do not. Some Christians donate generously to the church, others less so. Some go to a pilgrimage, most do not. And so forth. Furthermore, while there are a growing number of modern churches (Free Churches and independent churches) with no official ordination into ministry, virtually all Christian churches have designated pastors, ministers, or other leaders.

Although the Prophet Muhammad was but a human being, particularly in folk Islam and forms of Sufism his status is elevated to that of a (semi-)divine object of veneration. Sufi mysticism also has a number of saints similarly elevated, particularly Ali (even among the Sunnis). Somewhat similarly among the Christians, the older Christian traditions honor Mary, the Mother of God, and certain saints are honored although not worshipped as worship belongs only to God. That said, in some folk Christian circles, the borderline between the honoring and worshipping of Mary is thin, at times dangerously thin!

In Islam as in other religions, the annual life cycle follows the religious calendar, starting from the honoring of the date when Muhammad migrated from Mecca to Medina. Friday is not considered a holy day, although it is the day of congregation. Instead, a number of other holy days commemorate significant days in the life of the Prophet and early *ummah*. Globalization has caused much diversity in rituals and rites, but not in doctrine and prayers. Again, with all the differences, the presence of the life cycle bears resemblance to that in Christianity and in most other living faith traditions.

Having now considered the history, developments, and main features of the nature and life of the Islamic community alongside some comparative notes, it is useful to delve into some important case studies connecting and separating the two communities, the *ummah* and the church. Let us begin with the question as to what is Islam's relation to the two other Abrahamic cousin faiths. Thereafter, the missionary nature of Islam and its implications to Christian mission and coexistence will be considered, including the question of conversion.

Islam and Other Faith Communities

Islam's anchoring in the theological heritage of two older Abrahamic traditions explains its unique relation to them among all other faiths, even if its outlook at large is universal, similarly to that of Christianity (but much less so in Judaism). Echoing biblical theology, the Qur'an teaches that "'to God belongs the kingdom (*mulk*) of the heavens and earth' (e.g., 2:107)."[2] In this light it is understandable that Islam maintains a strong missionary impulse, to be discussed in the following section.

The unique relationship to Christianity and Judaism is clearly taught in Muslim Scripture. The Qur'an instructs us that "had God willed, He would have made them one community" (Q 42:8).[3] The general con-

2. Woodberry, "Kingdom of God," 49.

3. See also Q 42:10: "And whatever you may differ in, the verdict therein belongs

sensus is that the Abrahamic communities are meant here—although, it seems to me that even the rest of the humankind could also be the reference as far as the very earliest times of the emerging *ummah* is concerned. Recall the above-quoted passage in 10:19: "Mankind was but one community; then they differed." Be that as it may, the close affinity with Abrahamic communities is clearly and unequivocally taught in passages such as Q 42:15: "God is our Lord and your Lord. Our deeds concern us and your deeds concern you. There is no argument between us and you. God will bring us together, and to Him is the [final] destination."

In this light it is understandable that the earliest Qur'anic passages were not calling people to convert to a new religion; rather, the Meccans were called to "worship the Lord of this House [Ka'ba]" (Q 106:3).[4] Only later, with the rising opposition from the worshippers of local deities, was a decisive break announced, and the confession became "There is no god except God" (Q 37:35). We know that in Medina the Prophet with his companions lived among the Jews, and we may safely infer that he assumed that the new faith was in keeping with theirs as well as most probably with the Christian faith:

> O Children of Israel, remember My favour wherewith I favoured you; and fulfil My covenant, and I shall fulfil your covenant; and have awe of Me. And believe in what I have revealed, confirming that which is with you; and be not the first to disbelieve in it. And do not sell My signs for a small price; and fear Me (Q 2:40–41).

Recall also that at that time the term *muslim* could also be applied to non-Muslims, such as to Solomon (Q 27:44[5]) and disciples of Jesus (Q 3:52[6]). Only when the Jews rejected the Prophet was the direction of Muslims' prayer orientation changed from Jerusalem to Mecca (Q 2:149–50[7]).

---

to God. That then is God, my Lord; in Him I have put my trust, and to Him I turn penitently."

4. The Ka'ba, in Mecca, is the holiest place in Islam.

5. "She said, 'My Lord, indeed I have wronged myself, and I submit with Solomon to God, the Lord of the Worlds'" (Q 27:44). The female speaker here is the queen of Sheba.

6. "And when Jesus sensed their disbelief, he said, 'Who will be my helpers unto God?' The disciples said, 'We will be helpers of God; we believe in God; witness that we have submitted'" (Q 3:52).

7. "From whatever place you issue, turn your face towards the Sacred Mosque [in Mecca; my addition]; it is the truth from your Lord. God is not heedless of what you

The importance of the special status assigned to Abrahamic cousins is also illustrated in that between what the Muslims call "the Abode of Peace and the Abode of War," a third region was acknowledged, "the Abode of the People of the Book," that is, Jews and Christians. These two traditions enjoy a unique relation to Islam (Q 2:135–36):

> And they say, "Be Jews or Christians, and you shall be guided." Say, "Nay, rather the creed of Abraham, a hanīf; and he was not of the idolaters." Say: "We believe in God, and in that which has been revealed to us, and revealed to Abraham, Ishmael, Isaac, Jacob, and the Tribes, and that which was given to Moses, and Jesus, and the prophets, from their Lord, we make no division between any of them, and to Him we submit."

A justified implication might be that in some real sense the diversity of religions is not only tolerated by Allah but even planned and endorsed, at least when it comes to those who are the "People of the Book." "If God had willed, He would have made you one community, but that He may try you in what He has given to you. So vie with one another in good works; to God you shall all return, and He will then inform you of that in which you differed" (Q 5:48).[8]

This inclusive tendency towards Judaism and Christianity notwithstanding, Islam retains a unique place in God's eyes, Muslims argue. There is similarity here to contemporary Roman Catholic inclusivism: while other nations might have known God, only Muslims know Allah intimately and are most rightly related to God. That is most probably the meaning of the Qur'anic statements that Muslims, in distinction from others, are "God's sincere servants" (Q 37:40) and "they are of the elect, the excellent" (Q 38:47). Therefore, ultimately even Jewish and Christian traditions suffer from corruption and misunderstanding of the final revelation.

---

do. From whatever place you issue, turn your face towards the Sacred Mosque; and wherever you may be, turn your faces towards it, so that there be not any argument from the people against you; excepting the evildoers among them; and do not fear them, but fear Me; and that I may perfect My grace upon you, and that you may be guided" (Q: 2:149–50).

8. See also Q 3:113–15: "Yet they are not all alike; some of the People of the Scripture are a community upright, who recite God's verses in the watches of the night, prostrating themselves. They believe in God and in the Last Day, enjoining decency and forbidding indecency, vying with one another in good works; those are of the righteous. And whatever good they do, they shall not be denied it, and God knows the God-fearing."

Mission and Conversions

What distinguishes Islam and Christianity among all living faith traditions is that both of them are programmatically and actively missionary by their very nature. Apart from early Theravada Buddhism, that is not the case with others—notwithstanding some occasional attempts by, for example, some individual Hindu movements to convert non-Hindus or re-convert those who have left faith.

Even Judaism is not a missionary religion in any active sense, despite the fact that many Old Testament passages can be interpreted (at least by Christian readers) in terms of Yahweh having mandated the people of Israel to spread the knowledge of the one and only God. One is Jew by birth (from a Jewish mother). Something similar relates to the typical Hindu. One is Hindu by being born in India or to Indian parents in diaspora. Buddhism, as well, both in its current mainstream Mahayana form and the minority Theravada form, has lost the missionary impulse with only some occasional exceptions.

The main reason for the missionary nature of Islam is that, like Christianity's, Islam's outlook is universal, as discussed above. The *ummah* as an active missionary community is based on the Qu'ranic mandate to reach out to nonbelievers (Q 16:125).

> Call to the way of your Lord with wisdom and fair exhortation, and dispute with them by way of that which is best. Truly your Lord knows best those who stray from His way and He knows best those who are guided.

This verse also reminds the Muslims of the correct attitude in evangelizing and calling to repentance of unbelievers. It also sticks with what is clearly taught in the Qur'an, namely that conversion should be a matter of one's own choice, as "There is no compulsion in religion" (Q 2:256). This is not to deny—similar to Christian history—that there have been forced conversions, but those have to be considered anomalies rather than the norm.

The missionary mandate is often expressed with the Arabic term *da'wah*, literally "call" or "summons." It is "used especially in the sense of the religious outreach or mission to exhort people to embrace Islam as the true religion . . . In the modern period, *da'wah* most often refers to Islamic missionary activities, which are increasingly characterized by long-range planning, skillful exploitation of the media, establishment of study centers and mosques, and earnest, urgent preaching and efforts at persuasion."[9]

Combining a universalizing tendency and fervent missionary mandate, Islam's goal of outreach is comprehensive, including ideally social, economic, cultural, and religious spheres. In keeping with this vision,

> From North Africa to Indonesia, and beyond, Muslim individuals and organizations are strenuously dedicated to missionary activities, utilizing the media and other advanced means of communication and "market research." *Da'wah* faculties are prominent in Muslim training schools and universities, and the hope is that the strong obligation to spread Islam will be felt by Muslims at all levels of society. *Da'wah*, as well as migration, is responsible for the significant recent growth of Muslim populations in Western countries.[10]

Conversion to Islam entails confession of two simple but necessary convictions: that Allah is the only god and that Muhammad is the prophet of God—a confession usually recited in Arabic and followed by "the greater ablution" of the whole body. Part of the conversion process is an ongoing mindset of penitence and contrition, although there are no mandatory formal rites or rituals. Ritual prayers and *zakat*, "almsgiving" (9:5, 11); and submission (*islam*) to God (39:54) accompany the internal process of remorse and repentance.

What is strictly forbidden, however, is any Muslim's conversion to another religion, an apostasy potentially resulting in punishment by death.

> Conversion by Muslims to other faiths is forbidden under most interpretations of sharia and converts are considered apostates (non-Muslims, however, are allowed to convert into Islam). Some Muslim clerics equate this apostasy to treason, a crime punishable by death. The legal precedent stretches back to the seventh century when Prophet Mohammed ordered a Muslim man to death who joined the enemies of Islam at a time of war. However, because apostasy is not a crime under the criminal codes of Muslim states, generally the *murtad* (apostate) is not subject to any criminal sanction.[11]

9. Denny, "Da'wah," 2225.

10. Denny, "Da'wah," 2225–26. See also Ammar, "Principles of Dawah"; Ahmad and Kerr, eds., *Christian Mission and Islamic Da'wah*.

11. Beehner, "Religious Conversion."

Here there is a radical difference from contemporary Christianity, which allows personal judgment in matters of religion. While some smaller groups of Christians may try to pressure against changing one's religion, there is no scriptural or later teaching forbidding it under sentence of death.

Ultimately, *da'wah*, reaching out to the unbelievers, would result in the establishment of sharia law and gathering of all peoples under one *ummah*. No wonder, then, that during various historical eras, *da'wah* has been exercised with the help of military and political means—although, as mentioned, the Qur'an prohibits evangelism by force. Yet, alliances with earthly powers, militarism, and economic interests were all employed to spread Islam with force and brutality. In other words, not only Christianity but also Islam bears the long legacy of colonialism.

This takes us to the difficult issue of Islam's desire to introduce Sharia law as a part of its totalizing mission effort.

Sharia Law for All Peoples?

Comparison with the oldest Abrahamic tradition sets the stage for our discussion of Islamic Sharia law. Similarly to Judaism, Islam sees "the appropriate way to human fulfillment in obedience to a divinely revealed law," named in that tradition as the Sharia, which differs from Judaism in that it is "given to be followed by all humanity, and not just by one special community."[12]

How does Christian mission relate to that claim? Instead of a divinely given law to govern all of life as in a theocracy, Christian mission aims at providing a holistic way of life based on love of God and neighbor, leaving open issues of government (most inclusively understood). The attempts to coerce Christian "theocracy" on the pagan or even Christianized societies started early from the establishment of the Christendom alliance between the church and the earthly powers, but is nowadays widely condemned by all churches.

From a Christian perspective, it is highly ironic that the Islamic pursuit of global Sharia has from the beginning been closely allied with a specific ethnicity and language (Arabic) and, in modern and contemporary times, often with nationalism, particularly in the regions of the world colonized by European powers. How would a universal reach to

12. Ward, *Religion and Community*, 31.

all humanity be reconciled with that? "If Islam is indeed meant to be a global community, then it is self-defeating for Islam to oppose 'the West,' when Westerners should be Muslims too, and when many are."[13]

That said, sadly, both Islam and Christianity carry a legacy of colonialism as part of their mission histories. Unbeknownst to many, "While from the first there were considerable numbers of Christians under Muslim rule, yet until the appearance of European colonialism there were virtually no Muslims under Christian rule except for limited periods."[14] Everywhere where Christians lived under Muslim rule, the Sharia law totally forbade Christian sharing of the gospel with Muslims. Indeed, according to Sharia law, the penalty for apostasy—the Islamic perception of converting to Christianity—is death.

Let us complete this lengthier chapter with a brief look at the development and state of Muslim-Christian relations, as that is an essential issue in the comparison of these, currently the two biggest religious communities in the world.

Taking Stock of Muslim-Christian Relations

Not only does Judaism stand in a unique position in relation to the Christian church, so does Islam, albeit differently. That said, it is too rarely appreciated how different the Christianity first encountered by the Prophet and the early Muslim *ummah* was from the global Christian church today. In the seventh century, notwithstanding internal differences, there was one undivided church (at least formally).

Importantly, the segments of the church that early Islam engaged were either marginal or heretical in the eyes of the mainstream Christianity, namely, advocates of Nestorianism (which seemed to separate too robustly the two natures of Christ, the human and divine) and monophysitism (which was seen as erring on the opposite end of the spectrum, namely virtually subsuming the human under the divine). Most ironically, many of the objections of Muslims against the orthodox Christian doctrine of the Trinity and Christology either stem from or are strongly flavored by these Christian divergences.

On the one hand, Christian-Muslim encounters throughout history have been characterized by misperceptions, misrepresentations, and even

13. Ward, *Religion and Community*, 33.

14. Watt, *Muslim-Christian Encounters*, 74.

hostility. On the other hand, more often than not there has been more tolerance than would be expected from, say, cultures of the Middle Ages. There was also a shift in Christian perception: whereas for Christian apologists from the seventh and eighth century, such as John of Damascus, to the late medieval period, Islam was represented more like a heresy, from the late medieval period onward it was taken as a false religion.

Nowadays, a number of promising signs indicate that concerted efforts are underway to continue constructive mutual engagement, heal memories, and improve understanding of the two faiths. Recall the wise words from the Roman Catholic Vatican II's document on other religions, *Nostra Aetate*:

> The Church regards with esteem also the Moslems. They adore the one God, living and subsisting in Himself; merciful and all-powerful, the Creator of heaven and earth, who has spoken to men; they take pains to submit wholeheartedly to even His inscrutable decrees, just as Abraham, with whom the faith of Islam takes pleasure in linking itself, submitted to God. Though they do not acknowledge Jesus as God, they revere Him as a prophet. They also honor Mary, His virgin Mother; at times they even call on her with devotion.[15]

The common basis of these two faiths in monotheism, scriptural heritage, doctrine of creation, theological anthropology, eschatology, and the person of Jesus has been detailed above, and it alone mandates ongoing dialogue. Commonalities and differences also come to the surface in the missional orientation of both traditions.

It is encouraging that a number of dialogues, common study projects, and other processes seeking for a better mutual understanding and recognition are underway. It is yet to be seen what the final harvest of these many attempts might be for the future of relations between the world's two largest religious communities.

15. Vatican Council II, *Nostra Aetate*, para. 3.

11

What Will Happen at the "End"?

Orientation: The Expectation of the "End" Among Religions—and Elsewhere!

In all living religions there are visions of the future and the final "end"—as distinct as they might be. But not only among religions: the expectation, or at times fear, of the end can also be found in the secular realm. Consider, for example, the growing concern, at times anxiety, in secular culture and scientific study over the impending "end" either of our planet or of human life on earth. Natural catastrophe and the nuclear threat alone trigger all kinds of conjectures and fantasies. In other words, as integral as the visions of the "end" might be for religions, in no way are they limited to the sacred sphere alone!

In theological jargon, the expectation of and visions for the "end" and final consummation is named as eschatology, or the doctrine of the last things. Eschatology was first called in Latin "the last things" (from Latin *de novissimis*), and it simply referred to what was believed to happen at the end of human life and the world.

As the native English speaker knows, the term "end" is a polyvalent term. It can mean both completion (that is, coming or bringing to an end) and fulfillment (as in having reached the goal). Both meanings are present in the Christian eschatological expectation.

In traditional Christian theology, eschatology included the doctrine of "the four last things": death, judgment, hell, and heaven (including limbo, the place of blessedness for the unbaptized infants, and purgatory, the Catholic idea of the needed purification of those on the way to their final bliss). In contemporary theology, issues related to the resurrection of the body, the "intermediate state" (that is, the "interval" between the personal death and final eschatological consummation, if any), and the fate and destiny of our planet and the whole cosmos are also in view.

When put in the wider context of religions, "In its broadest sense the term 'eschatology' includes all concepts of life beyond death and everything connected with it such as heaven and hell, paradise and immortality, resurrection and transmigration of the soul, rebirth and reincarnation, and last judgment and doomsday."[1] Accordingly, although the Christian theologian has to be careful when speaking of "eschatology" as a pan-religious theme, it is true that all world religions express a concern over death and the end of our lives and the life of the whole cosmos eventually. As diverse as these beliefs and symbols may be, it is clear that some kind of common denominator exists.

Eschatology is particularly important for the Abrahamic faiths, for two reasons. First, their conception of time is linear. This naturally inclines toward the idea of the beginning and the end, an assumption foreign to great Asiatic faiths, to whom time is cyclical. Rather than a definite beginning and end, both Buddhist and Hindu thinking envision endless beginnings and endings. Second, Judaism, Christianity, and Islam are guardians of robust "theistic" religious tradition. This means that from the very beginning to the very end the one and only God is the one who brings about everything, cares and caters for everything, and is believed to bring to completion God's eternal purposes. Again, this is markedly different from Asiatic faiths, in which no doctrine of creation, and hence, no Creator God, is to be found; commensurately, the final "end" is not the sovereign work of God or any of the many deities. On the contrary, gods are also subject to the cycle of emergence and disappearance.

Notwithstanding these foundational similarities among the three Abrahamic cousins, there are also differences with regard to eschatology. Briefly stated, Judaism is the "least" eschatologically oriented tradition as far as the focus of the doctrine of the last things is concerned. For Israel's and the ensuing (Rabbinic) Judaism's religion it took a long time for any kind of definite visions, let alone stated doctrines, of eschatology

1. Schwarz, *Eschatology*, 26.

to emerge, because its outlook is robustly this-worldly. Rather than in the distant future, Yahweh's blessings—long age, progeny, and riches—are to be had and enjoyed in this life, the final crowning of which is an honorable burial among the "fathers." The nature of death was some kind of shadowy existence in the darkness and the whole idea of eternal life (beyond life on this earth) appeared only slowly.

Not so in Islam, where eschatology including death, judgment, heaven, and hell in the "beyond" is a leading spiritual and theological motif. Eschatology lays claim on the whole faith and life of the Muslim. Islamic faith in comparison to Judaism is very much other-worldly oriented.

Christian tradition oscillates in between these two poles. On the one hand, in contrast to Judaism, there is a definite future-oriented eschatological undergirding and expectation. On the other hand, learning from Israel's faith and in contrast to Islam, Christian faith seeks to balance the this-worldly and other-worldly orientations. With the exception of the very first centuries (and some present-day marginal groups), high-level enthusiasm for the "end" is not the hallmark of Christian communities.

Before we get into many details of Islam's rich eschatology, a recap of the Christian vision of the last things is important. Thereafter, we are ready for some detailed comparative work.

The Christian Eschatological Vision

Based on the intense expectation of the final coming of God's kingdom among the earliest followers of Jesus Christ, the patristic church was preparing for the appearance of the world-to-come and for the final resolution or consummation of all things. Although this eschatological hope waned somewhat after the establishment of Christendom in the fourth century, as a result of which Christianity became more or less a state-promoted religion, in no way did the future orientation die out. Indeed, more often than not, particularly in the Middle Ages and all the way to the Reformation era, eschatological imagination fueled spirituality.

Even if in the hands of the academic Enlightenment critics, other-worldly expectation of divine intervention at the end of the world became suspicious and often rejected, the doctrine of the last things did not die out. The expectation of the "end" rather became more varied and even more comprehensive.

Similarly to the issues of origins (the doctrine of creation), contemporary Christian eschatology has to take into consideration the conjectures of natural sciences concerning the fate of our planet, life, and the cosmos. This also creates a tension because, according to the predictions of the sciences, all life and matter will ultimately come to an end and finally lead to nil, whereas in theological eschatology God is bringing about the "new heaven and new earth." Indeed, what makes Christian eschatology distinctive among religions is that it encompasses all of creation, not only humans, nor merely Earth, but also the whole vast cosmos. That said, it took a long time for Christian theology to consider the many implications of this wide horizon. Understandably, in early Christian theology personal (and "human") eschatology became the focus of the Christian hope.

At the center of Christian eschatology is the hope for the bodily resurrection in the new creation, a hope that keeps in dynamic tension continuity and discontinuity between this life and life eternal. For any kind of future embodied life in personal communion with God and other human beings to make sense, it needs some kind of correspondence with the conditions of current embodied life. The two other Abrahamic faiths also share some kind of idea of the resurrection of the body, but it hardly stands at the center in either Islam or Judaism.

Ultimately, as with all Christian topics, so also with the resurrection of the body: Christ is the key. His resurrection from the dead is the foundation. St. Paul labors on this point in 1 Corinthians 15, arguing that Christ's resurrection forms the basis for Christian hope (1 Cor 15:14). Indeed, the apostle goes so far as to claim that had Christ not been raised, Christian faith would be futile and there would be no hope for eternal life (vv. 17–19). Christ was raised to new life by the Father through the Holy Spirit (Rom 1:4). As a result, the indwelling Spirit in believers constantly reminds them of the certainty of their own resurrection by the same Spirit who raised Christ (Rom. 8:11).

As there are so many shared themes—from death, to intermediate state (the interval between each person's physical death to the final consummation), to heaven and hell, to the signs of the end, and to judgment—it is useful to highlight the Christian position alongside a discussion of Islamic eschatology.

Why the End-Time Expectation Plays Such a Big Role in Islam

As mentioned, eschatology plays an extraordinary role in Islam. The Prophet's first and continuing message was about the coming judgment and the need for everyone to submit to Allah to avoid hell. For the Muslim, life on this earth is but preparation for eternity, at the core of which is obedience to and desire to please Allah.

Indeed, it is the life to come that is "real"—or more real—than the short lifespan on earth, as the Qur'an teaches: "And the life of this world is nothing but diversion and play. But surely the Abode of the Hereafter is indeed the [true] Life, if they only knew" (Q 29:64). Whereas life on Earth is only temporary, the afterlife lasts forever: "Nay, but you prefer the life of this world, whereas the Hereafter is better and more lasting" (Q 87:16–17).

Hence, death should be appropriately kept in mind: having first narrated the way the human person was initially created, this terse statement in the Qur'an 23:15 hastens to add that "Then indeed after that you die" (Q 23:15). In fact, each human has been given a stated life span, "A term is stated with Him . . ." (Q 6:2). The reality of death lays claim on whole life because of the stark difference between different destinies:

> Every soul shall taste of death; you shall surely be paid in full your wages on the Day of Resurrection. Whoever is moved away from the Fire and admitted to Paradise, will have triumphed, the life of this world is but the comfort of delusion (Q 3:185).

Both the Qur'an and particularly Hadith texts go to great lengths in discussing the afterlife. Eschatological beliefs are also prominent in many Muslim creedal statements. Generally speaking, contemporary Muslims tend to take the traditional teaching on eschatology much more seriously than do most Jews and Christians. Not surprisingly, similarly to Judaism and Christianity, although even more robustly, radical millenarian and jihadist movements with all kinds of fantasies of the end, including the use of violence in God's name, find fertile soil among Muslims in various global locations.[2]

2. An interested reader may consult my essay, Kärkkäinen, "Hope Gone Awry."

Looking for the Signs of the "Hour"

As in Christian tradition, in Islam the (final) hour is unknown to all but God (Q 31:34[3]). The Prophet stated: "Knowledge thereof lies only with God—and what do you know, perhaps the Hour is near" (33:63). Differently from Hadith and apocalyptic traditions, the Qur'an is reticent to talk about signs. That said, eschatological undergirding lies beneath a number of suras, such as sura 22, with the opening verse: "O mankind, fear your Lord. Surely the earthquake of the Hour [of Doom] is a tremendous thing."

Understandably, Muslims have not stopped looking for signs of the end. Books, blogs, and talks on "signs of the hour" abound. The search for signs is fueled by the presence in the Hadith of detailed lists of signs. "Geological, moral, social, and cosmic signs . . . [as well as] the erosion of the earth, the spread of immorality, the loss of trust among people, and the administration of unjust rulers [are perceived] as some signs of the Hour." In distinction from these "minor" signs, the Hadith lists as "major" ones the "emergence of the Antichrist, the descent of Jesus, and the rising of the sun from the west," which all point to the imminence of the end.[4] Quite similarly to the descriptions in the book of Revelation, trumpets, archangels, and cataclysmic changes on earth, including earthquakes, play a role in the final consummation and the unfaithful will suffer intensely. The rise of the mysterious nations of Gog and Magog also plays a role in the eschatological scheme of Islam.[5]

Obviously, the search for signs and their general nature resembles greatly that in Christian tradition, including also the signs of the coming of the antichrist, to be discussed in the next subsection. Curiously, but understandably, despite the repeated reservation of Jesus against paying much attention to them (see Matt 12:38–39, 24:36, for example), beginning from the New Testament times the interest in discerning, and more often than not determining, the signs of the end has been quite popular among Christians. In fact, at every critical juncture of historical events the "end" has been proclaimed and time after time the prediction has so far shown to be mistaken!

3. "Lo! God, with Him lies knowledge of the Hour; and He sends down the rain, and He knows what is in the wombs. And no soul knows what it will earn tomorrow, and no soul knows in what land it will die. Truly God is Knower, Aware" (Q 31:34).

4. Saritoprak, *Islam's Jesus*, 38–39.

5. Saritoprak, *Islam's Jesus*, 39, 45.

That said, a cautious and discerning scrutiny of signs is not discouraged in the New Testament. Just note that while the basic profile of the signs in Christian eschatology is quite similar to that in Islam there are two important differences. First of all, there are at least two distinctive end-time signs in Christianity, namely the proclamation of the gospel unto the whole world and the gathering of the Jewish people back to their homeland. Neither one of them is found in Islam. Second, the focus of Christians' search for signs is not on the end times *per se*, although that is also the case, but rather in the return of Jesus Christ! Even when Jesus plays a role in Islamic expectations, as will be discussed below, his role is far from that in Christian faith as the center of all expectations.

Jesus and Mahdi, the Central End-Time Players—Alongside the Antichrist

Here we come to one of the most distinctive features of Islamic eschatological expectations! Unbeknownst to most Christians, Jesus plays a noteworthy role in Islamic eschatology. Furthermore, the main player in the end-time drama is the mysterious figure of the Mahdi, whose deputy Jesus is.

But why Jesus? What has he to do with Islam's end-time events? Recall that, as discussed in chapters 4 and 7, according to the standard Islamic interpretation, Jesus of Nazareth was not killed on the cross but was instead "taken up" by Allah to heaven to await his return (Q 4:157–58). On top of that, keep in mind the profound status and role of Jesus in Islamic faith at large. In that light, the idea of him appearing also as an eschatological actor is not, in fact, so strange at all. In the words of a leading Muslim scholar:

> Since the early period of Islam, Muslims have read the sayings of the Prophet, referred to as Hadith, about Jesus and the end-time scenario, finding nothing strange about Jesus's praying in a mosque. Muslims see no incongruity between Jesus and the mosque since the Prophet Muhammad and Jesus are considered spiritual brothers. This clearly indicates that Muslims have honored Jesus as a part of their faith and culture. Perhaps for this reason many adherents of Islamic faith name their children 'Isa, the Qur'anic name for Jesus.[6]

6. Saritoprak, *Islam's Jesus*, xiii.

In fact, notwithstanding the lack of direct references to the descent of Jesus in the Qur'an, some key statements about his work and meaning have been interpreted as having important eschatological implications. Consider, for example, Q 3:46 ("He shall speak to mankind in the cradle, and in his manhood, and he is of the righteous"), which can be interpreted to refer to the future ("he *shall* speak") in terms of Jesus' ministry yet unfinished. In the Hadith tradition, Q 43:61[7] has played a role. This passage is in the context of the people of Mecca contesting for the superiority of their gods (or angels?), in response to which the Prophet lifted up the role of Jesus as the sign of the hour.[8] Furthermore, it is noteworthy that in the Hadith, Jesus is figured as handsome and clean, "symbolic of his pure message and of the mission to be fulfilled." Jesus appears there as the one much loved and supported by the Muslims.[9]

What about the Mahdi? His task is to defeat the antichrist and bring justice and peace to the world and lead people to truth. An ordinary human being rather than a divine figure, the Mahdi is supernaturally endowed to accomplish his task. What is strange about the Mahdi is that he is not mentioned in the Qur'an at all nor in the two main Hadith traditions, that of Bukhari and of Muslim. Yet, he is affirmed by all major denominations, although his role is particularly important among the Shi'ites.

The relationship between the Mahdi and Jesus is close yet somewhat undefined. Jesus will fight alongside the Mahdi against the antichrist and defeat him. Jesus will slaughter pigs, tear down crosses, and destroy churches and synagogues; most probably he will also kill Christians unwilling to embrace Islamic faith.

Alongside these two major protagonists, a narrative which differs radically from the Christian story and cannot be reconciled with it, there is the third figure which is much more familiar to Christians, namely the antichrist. Its picture in Islam is not radically different from that in Christianity. Obviously an archenemy of Jesus, the antichrist can be seen as the personification of evil (similarly to Satan, Iblis). Although the term *antichrist* itself does not appear in the Qur'an, there is wide agreement in Islamic tradition that allusions and indirect references are found in it, including the saying attributed to Jesus: "Nay, but verily man is [wont to be] rebellious" (Q 96:6).

7. "And indeed he is a portent of the Hour so do not doubt it but: 'Follow me. This is a straight path'" (Q 43:61).

8. Saritoprak, *Islam's Jesus*, 27–28.

9. Saritoprak, *Islam's Jesus*, 77.

Understandably, the Hadith traditions greatly expand and elaborate on the description and influence of the antichrist: "The Antichrist is short, hen-toed, woolly-haired, one-eyed, an eye-sightless, and neither protruding nor deep-seated. If you are confused about him, know that your Lord is not one-eyed."[10] The antichrist will fight against the believers until the Mahdi and Jesus come and help defeat his power.

Whereas the figure of antichrist plays a role in Christian tradition, there are only a few scattered references to the figure. In the biblical testimonies (such as 2 Thess 2:3–12), he is depicted as "a universal ruler whose reign of unprecedented evil . . . Christ will defeat at his parousia."[11] Clearly, there are here echoes from the fall narrative's mention of the desire to "be like God" (Gen 3:5). The fact alone that the guesswork about who the antichrist is has always proven to be wrong should discourage Christians from paying too much attention to this mysterious and "hidden" figure. Instead, the focus should be on Christ and what the triune God is doing in working out cosmic destiny according to his own plans unknown to us.

Death and Resurrection

What is distinctive about the Islamic conception of death is the experience of torment and pain in the grave prior to judgment and resurrection. The term used in Islam to refer to this period is *barzakh*, "the physical barrier between the Garden and the Fire or between this world and the life beyond the grave, as well as the period of time separating individual death and final resurrection."[12] That said, the Qur'an itself provides precious few details about what happens between death and resurrection. Here is an apt summary of its main teachings:

> [I]n S[ura] 56:82 we are told that the soul of the dying person comes up to his throat, and in S 6:93 death is described as a kind of flooding-in process [*ghamarāt al-maut*] at which time angels stretch forth their hands and ask that the souls be given over to them. Exactly what happens after that the Qur'ān does not say, although the traditions describe the succeeding events elaborately. Again, the only clue in the Qur'ān as to whether or not the dead have any degree of consciousness is the indication

10. *Sunan Abi Dawud*, Book 39, Hadith 30.

11. Bauckham and Hart, *Hope against Hope*, 110–11.

12. Smith, "Reflections," 92n4.

> in S 35:22 that the living and the dead are not alike, and that while God can accord hearing to whomever He wills, the living cannot make those in the graves hear them.[13]

It is left to later traditions to develop fairly detailed accounts. While not without internal debates, the basic outline of what happens at and immediately after death is fairly straightforward. Similarly to Christian tradition, those accounts say that whereas the body decays, the "soul" (or "spirit") continues to exist.[14]

According to a major Muslim tradition, the deceased person meets two angels—most often named Munkar and Nakir—who test the faith of the person and help determine that person's final destiny. There is also a widely spread folk belief among the Muslims that alongside these two angels, there might be others, including the mysterious Angel of Death. But these are not universally held beliefs,

Following the questioning and punishment in the grave, it is widely assumed that some kind of state of unconsciousness will follow until the day of resurrection. The most typical description of this unconscious state is sleep, a metaphor well known in other Abrahamic faiths as well.[15] One important Qur'anic verse is routinely invoked as the scriptural basis for this belief (Q 39:42):

> God takes the souls at the time of their death, and, those that have not died in their sleep. Then He retains those for whom He has ordained death and releases the others until an appointed term. Truly in that there are signs for a people who reflect.

For the Christian reader, it might be interesting to know that among Muslims, there is also a widespread belief in Satan visiting the dying person. This tempter's main goal is to urge the person to give up her or his faith in God and so snatch away the person from a blissful eternal destiny. A typically vivid description of this moment goes like this: "The person in this condition is generally described as suffering from an intense thirst and burning of the liver. Satan, not surprisingly, comes to the left side of the head and offers the agonized person a cup of cold water. The faithful

13. Smith and Haddad, *Islamic Understanding*, 32.

14. Q 39:42: "God takes the souls at the time of their death, and, those that have not died in their sleep. Then He retains those for whom He has ordained death and releases the others until an appointed term. Truly in that there are signs for a people who reflect."

15. Smith and Haddad, *Islamic Understanding*, 48–49.

believer cries out, 'Give me some water!' not seeing who is offering it, to which Satan replies, 'Say: The Prophet lied.'"[16] That said, it is also believed that the final destiny of the dying person is already sealed and that therefore this satanic temptation most likely will not make a change.

Not only does the Christian tradition offer fewer details about what it believes to happen at the moment of, and immediately following, death, the mainstream teaching knows no accompanying angelic figures, nor testing at the moment of death, including that by Satan. This is a notable difference between the two eschatologies.

Importantly, death, as irrevocable as it is, does not have the last word in Islam, an affirmation shared with other Abrahamic faiths. Muslims believe in the resurrection of the body: "Then indeed after that you die. Then on the Day of Resurrection you shall surely be raised" (Q 23:15–16). In the sura 75, named "The Rising of the Dead," there is a rhetorical question "Does man suppose that We shall not assemble his bones?" to which the awaited answer is: "Yes, indeed! We are able to reshape [even] his fingers!" (vv. 3, 4).

Based on numerous scriptural and later traditional teachings, Muslims hold firmly to the hope of resurrection:

> The promise, the guarantee, of the day at which all bodies will be resurrected and all persons called to account for their deeds and the measure of their faith is the dominant message of the Qur'ān as it is presented in the context of God's *tawḥīd*. One can find testimony of this assurance on almost every page of the Qur'ān.[17]

According to the mainstream teaching, Muhammad (who is, recall, not a divine figure but rather the conduit of divine teaching) will be the first among the resurrected ones. A related major tradition teaches that major prophets follow in his footsteps. "The stress on the importance of Muḥammad's resurrection before the other believers is related not only to his recognized stature as the seal of the prophets, but also to the general understanding of his role as intercessor for his community."[18]

The main theological debate about the resurrection is whether it entails a total annihilation of the person before re-creation or a reconstitution and renewal. The lack of unanimity is understandable in light of

16. Smith and Haddad, *Islamic Understanding*, 38.
17. Smith and Haddad, *Islamic Understanding*, 63.
18. Smith and Haddad, *Islamic Understanding*, 73.

two kinds of directions in Scripture itself. Compare Q 28:88, "Everything will perish except His Countenance," which clearly assumes the annihilationist view, with Q 10:4, "To Him is the return of all of you . . . Truly He originates creation, then recreates it," which teaches the other option. Even during the most meticulous debates among the leading medieval Muslim philosophers and theologians no unanimity was found.

While the belief in bodily resurrection is a shared belief with Islam, the Christian expectation is totally focused on Christ and his bodily resurrection, an anathema to all Muslims. And while Christian faith is monotheistic, even the resurrection hope, as focused as it is on Christ, is ultimately triune: it is the Father who raises up the dead in the power of the Spirit in the footsteps of the One who was raised first, the Son.

When it comes to annihilation or reconstitution, Christian tradition has debated this issue for over two millennia. Without delving into those fairly complex disputes between parties, all of whom claim to have biblical support for their view, suffice to summarize this briefly: whereas the annihilation view had become fairly dominant by the time of the Protestant Reformation and even subsequently, in modern theology a dynamic mutuality between annihilation and (call it) transformation can be found. This seeks to do justice, on the one hand, to the goodness of God's creation and on the other hand, acknowledge the need for judgment and condemnation.

Here we come to a topic central to Islamic eschatology, namely judgment.

The Judgment Day

Final judgment is of great concern to Islam. Consider that a typical list of the basic beliefs includes "belief in one God, His messengers, His books, His angels, and the day of judgment."[19] The final accounting happens when in the hereafter men and women "return" to their God (32:11–12[20]). Numerous chapters of the Qur'an speak of or refer to the theme of judgment. Similarly to the New Testament, even the evil spirits (*jinn*) will be judged on that day.

19. Haleem, "Qur'an and Hadith," 25.

20. "Say: 'The Angel of death, who has been charged with you, shall receive you [in death], then to your Lord you shall be returned.' And if could you but see the guilty hanging their heads [low] before their Lord: 'Our Lord! We have seen and heard. So send us back so that we may act righteously, for indeed we are convinced'" (Q 32:11–12).

Above we noted that the first time the human person will be tested happens immediately following physical death and that there might be suffering and punishment for sin already in the grave. This means that, rightly and properly understood, we can speak of a two-stage judgment, the initial and the final one (at the eschaton). But rather than speaking of "two judgments," it is best to speak of a process of judgment culminating in the final and ultimate judgment.

Again, not surprisingly, there are a lot of commonalities between the Christian and Islamic vision of the day of judgment—going back to the Old Testament idea of the "day," a technical term referring to the end of times when evil and evil people(s) will be condemned and Yahweh's righteousness established. Commensurately, all three Abrahamic traditions refuse to give any kind of precise dating of the coming day. Only its inevitability in the future is strongly affirmed.

The general picture of the day of judgment is very similar to that given in the Bible. Mountains will be shaken (18:47) and various kinds of other dramatic cosmic events will take place. Sura 99, entitled "The Earthquake," speaks of the final judgment in terms of the time "When earth is shaken with its [final] quake," upheaval so big that "the earth brings forth its burdens," probably meaning that the graves will be opened (v. 1–2). And "On that day mankind shall issue forth in separate groups to be shown their deeds" (v. 6). According to Sura 82, entitled "Cleavage," it is the day

> When the heaven is split open, and when the stars are dispersed, and when the seas are burst forth, and when the tombs are overturned, [and then] a soul will know what it has sent ahead and left behind. (vv. 1–5)

On the day of judgment, men and women "shall be presented before your Lord in ranks . . . And the Book shall be set in place. And you will see the guilty apprehensive of what is in it, and they will say: 'O woe to us! What is it with this Book that it leaves out neither small nor great, but [instead it] has counted it?' And they shall find all that they did present. And your Lord does not wrong anyone (18:48–49)." On the left hand of God, so the tradition assumes, are the deeds of the condemned and on the right hand the faithful are blessed.

Islam's robust focus on the justice of Allah is based on frequent affirmations in the Qur'an, such as, "God created the heavens and the earth with the truth and so that every soul may be requited for what it has earned, and they will not be wronged" (45:22). This righteous and truthful judgment operates in the context of "balance" that "has been interpreted as the principle of justice and occasionally even the books through which the principles of justice are clarified." Underlying this term *balance* is of course weighing. A typical Muslim belief is that a couple of angels (usually Jibril and Mikhael) do the work of assessing the quality of one's life and faith in order to determine the end result.[21]

A debated issue among the Muslim schools is the lot of the (gravely) sinning believer, and no agreement has been reached about this. A related debate asks: How do the person's good and bad deeds account for the final judgment received? Common to all opinions is the centrality of obedience to Allah or lack thereof; furthermore, it is widely agreed that only grave sins bring about judgment.[22]

Two Destinies: Hell and Heaven

Similarly to traditional Judaism and Christianity, there is unanimous opinion across the Muslim denominations that there are two destinies taught in the Scripture:

> And the first to lead the way, of the Emigrants and the Helpers, and those who follow them by being virtuous, God will be pleased with them, and they will be pleased with Him; and He has prepared for them Gardens—with rivers flowing beneath them to abide therein forever: that is the supreme triumph. And among those around you of the Bedouins there are hypocrites, and among the townspeople of Medina, who are obstinate in hypocrisy. You do not know them but We know them, and We shall chastise them twice, then they will be returned to a terrible chastisement. And [there are] others, who have confessed their sins, they have mixed a righteous deed with another that was bad. It may be that God will relent to them. Truly God is Forgiving, Merciful. (Q 9:100–102; see also 7:37–51 and 75:20–25, among others)

Not surprisingly, Islamic tradition has unusually rich traditions about hell. It is a place of pain and torture, as graphically described both in the Qur'an and in later tradition: "Verily Hell lurks in ambush for the

21. Smith and Haddad, *Islamic Understanding*, 77.

22. Q 4:31: "If you avoid the grave sins that are forbidden you, We will absolve you of your evil deeds and admit you by an honourable gate."

rebellious [it is] a resort, to remain therein for ages, tasting in it neither coolness, nor drink, except boiling water and pus, as a fitting requital" (Q 78:21–26). The most frequent metaphor is that of fire: "Surely those who disbelieve in Our signs—We shall expose them to a Fire" (Q 4:56).

> The Qur'ān also gives a broad picture of the topography of Hell. It is an underground prison, always burning. The damned will enter humiliated, while Hell roars like a volcano (Q 68:7–8). Various punishments await the damned, who may be chained, forced to wear fiery garments, or pushed into the void, while boiling and stinking water is poured over them. They will also be forced to eat from trees . . . which bear fruits that torment them. Every attempt to improve their condition or to get help from believers will prove futile . . .[23]

What about heaven? Often depicted in the Qur'an with garden images, paradise is a place of great enjoyment, peace, and reunion. The Qur'an offers sensual descriptions, including the pleasures of exquisitely delicious food and drink, as well as of sexual relations with divine maidens (often interpreted metaphorically). Such a well-known description can be found in sura 37, which, having first delineated all the pains, torture, and suffering in hell, lays before our eyes this most beautiful description waiting for "God's sincere servants":

> For them there will be a distinct provision, fruits and they will be honoured in the Gardens of Bliss, [reclining] upon couches, facing one another; they are served from all round with a cup from a spring, white, delicious to the drinkers, wherein there is neither madness, nor will they be spent by it, and with them will be maidens of restrained glances with beautiful eyes, as if they were hidden eggs. (Q 37:40–49)

Particularly splendid and elaborate accounts of paradise ("Garden") can be found in the Hadith. Similarly to the Bible, there are also various levels of rewards for the blessed ones.

The Jewish and Christian reader finds a lot of common territory in Islam's description of both hell and heaven, although it has to be noted that in both of the older Abrahamic theologies, and particularly in the aftermath of the Enlightenment, deep disagreements about the necessity, nature, and credibility of the traditional notion of hell have arisen. Hence, neither modern Jewish nor modern Christian theology speaks

23. Tottoli, "Afterlife."

with one voice. The same applies to heaven: whereas for traditional theology the biblical perspectives on the final blessedness were taken more or less literally and were robustly future-oriented, in modern Christian theology there is a heavy debate between more this-worldly oriented and other-worldly oriented visions with no unanimity in purview. And as mentioned, for Jewish faith heaven as an other-worldly ultimate destiny has never been the main focus.

Be that as it may, a marked difference in relation to the Islamic view of both heaven and hell is that the Bible provides less detailed descriptions of both ultimate ends. Even when Jesus, as is well-known, mentions hell a number of times, his warnings are just that, namely *warnings* rather than explanations about what really happens or what kind of place hell might be. Something similar applies to heaven. The biggest difference is the sensual element totally missing in the biblical accounts, both of the Old and the New Testament. Other than that, the garden motif plays a vital role in Christian imagination of heaven; dominant is also the imagination related to the holy city, Jerusalem, and its safety and blessedness.

What about the fate non-Muslims? Whereas generally speaking, as has become clear by now, ignorance of Allah's revelation and refusal to submit certainly subject every person under the possibility of judgment and hell, there are also some inclusive views of salvation at the center of Islam's teaching when it comes to Abrahamic cousins: "Surely those who believe, and those of Jewry, and the Christians, and the Sabaeans,[24] whoever believes in God and the Last Day, and performs righteous deeds—their wage is with their Lord, and no fear shall befall them, neither shall they grieve" (Q 2:62). While the exact implications of this passage are of course widely debated among historical and contemporary Muslim scholars, there is no doubt that there is some kind of openness. Echoing the biblical view for those who have never heard the gospel, the Qur'an teaches that "We never punish until we have sent a messenger" (17:15, (Marmaduke Pickthall trans.).

Final Reflection on the Expectation of the End

Whereas Islam's eschatological vision shares many core beliefs of the Abrahamic cousin faiths, there is more similarity between Christian and

24. The Sabaeans (or Sabeans, Sabians; also in Q 5:69) are an obscure, little-known (old) Arabic-speaking tribe, also mentioned in the Old Testament (Joel 3:8; Isa 45:14).

Muslim visions than there is between the Muslim and Jewish visions, particularly with the important role played by Jesus Christ in the end-time events. That said, Jesus' role in Islamic eschatology is vastly different from his role in the Christian tradition. This issue is closely linked with the most distinctive Islamic conception, namely, the mysterious figure of the Mahdi. Subordinate and subservient to Mahdi, Jesus plays a role in Islam like that of a deputy, as opposed to Christian eschatology's assigning to him the main role in ushering in God's kingdom.

Although the belief in resurrection is affirmed in Islam, it seems its end-time vision is more otherworldly than that of the other two Abrahamic religions. That said, garden and city metaphors are also found therein, coupled with earthly types of pleasures, at least to the chosen ones, the martyrs.

All in all, eschatology plays a significantly more prominent role in Islam than in the two elder sister faiths. No wonder its contemporary apocalypticism and millenarianism are also fervent and at times even violent.

Epilogue

My late, beloved colleague at Fuller Theological Seminary, David Augsburger, professor of pastoral theology, helped coin a neologism, "interpathy," a shorthand for "inter-cultural empathy." With that word, David meant to say that you are willing *temporarily* to suspend your own beliefs, your own perspective, your own truth for the sake of inhabiting the space of the Other. You would be willing to step over the many cross-cultural obstacles on the way to encountering the Other as Other. And not just encountering but inhabiting the space of the Other without in any way violating the otherness of the Other.

This principle also embodies wonderfully well the attitude and posture towards encountering the religious Other. When a Muslim and a Christian meet, it is not only about the meeting of two religions. It is an encounter between two human persons, both of them created in the image of God. Notwithstanding deep and wide disagreements about who God is and what God has done, ultimately both the Muslim and the Christian seek truth, beauty, and value in life—and death.

Interpathy is another way of saying what yet another former Fuller colleague of mine, Miroslav Volf of Yale University, names "double vision." In his profound political-theological essay *Exclusion and Embrace*, Miroslav suggests that double vision allows us to look at the world and things from the perspective of the Other as well as from our own perspective. It lets the voices and experiences of the Other resonate with those of ours. Professor Volf himself comes from the war-stricken Balkans, where the

Christian difference (between the Catholics, Orthodox, and Protestants), cultural-linguistic difference, and the religious difference particularly between Christians and Muslims, has hindered peaceful encounters with the Other. Sadly, it has led to violence, war, and genocide. In that kind of environment, interpathy and double vision are truly needed!

Or think of the great Jewish philosopher Emmanuel Levinas's emphasis on seeing the face of the Other. In the face of the Other, we experience a kind of exodus from the limitations of our own perspective and its biases. We come changed out of the experience of seeing the face of the Other. And we can never explain away the identity of the Other because the face also represents infinity.

This short book has attempted to provide a platform for Christians and Muslims to come to a shared space and meet with each other. It is meant to facilitate conversation about deeply held religious beliefs that command common interest among these cousin faiths' adherents. Not that these doctrines—say Scripture, God, or the End—are similarly conceived; not at all. What I mean is that there is enough commonality to continue conversation! An added bonus: between the two younger Abrahamic cousins there is a wide and deep common base in the Scriptures of the people of Israel and in the traditions of (later) Judaism.

As discussed in the Introduction, a comparative exercise such as this one—written from a committed Christian standpoint—is not a "neutral," noncommittal exercise. It is confessional in that a believer in a particular faith tradition seeks to advance a reasonable and compelling argument on behalf of that tradition in a critical and sympathetic dialogue with others. Even though this kind of confessional comparative work is neither dogmatic nor closed-minded—as it functions best in a hospitable spirit—it also seeks to invite the religious Other to consider the truth and beauty of the Christian gospel. But doing so, it does not have to mock or ridicule Muslim faith and spirituality. This kind of hospitable invitation can be done in meekness and respect.

The existence of common scriptural and spiritual base not only makes meaningful a hospitable, respectful dialogue. In fact, it makes this kind of exchange both urgent and critical. As discussed above, much hangs on the relationship between these currently two largest living faith traditions. The fact that their adherents together comprise over half of the world's population should be a clarion call for a patient mutual understanding and learning. Indeed, the statistics are telling us that already in the near future the proportion of the global population by these two faiths may even increase! Hence, the stakes are even higher.

After so many centuries of persistent prejudice, unwillingness to listen to the Other, and the spreading of stereotypes—as still happens even in our days both in secular media and religious proclamation—both parties are called to embody humility and respect rather than pride and exclusion. Ultimately, a fruitful dialogue and encounter is a function of repentance and re-examination of our hearts and attitudes.

Speaking evil of the Other, presenting the Other's views in the worst possible ways, and relying on second-hand information about the Other block the way for mutual understanding and respect. Instead, as the current Roman Catholic papal pronouncement advises, there is a higher road ahead of us:

> An attitude of openness in truth and in love must characterize the dialogue with the followers of non-Christian religions, in spite of various obstacles and difficulties . . . Interreligious dialogue is a necessary condition for peace in the world, and so it is a duty for Christians as well as other religious communities . . . In this way we learn to accept others and their different ways of living, thinking and speaking.[1]

1. See Francis, *Evangelii Gaudium*, sec. 250.

Bibliography

Abrahams, Israel, Jacob Haberman, and Charles Manekin. "Belief." In *Encyclopedia Judaica*, edited by Michael Berenbaum and Fred Skolnik, 3:290–94. 2nd ed. 17 vols. Detroit: Macmillan Reference USA, 2007.

Ahmad, Khurshid, and David Kerr. *Christian Mission and Islamic Da'wah: Proceedings of the Chambésy Dialogue Consultation*. Leicester, UK: The Islamic Foundation, 1982.

Al-Azm, Sadiq Jalal. *Islam: Submission and Disobedience*. Vol. 2. Berlin: Gerlach, 2014.

Al-Busiri. *The Mantle Adorned*. Translated by Abdal Hakim Murad. London: Quilliam, 2009.

Al-Ghazzali. *The Alchemy of Happiness*. Translated by Claud Field. London: John Murray, 1910.

Ammar, Abu. "Principles of Dawah—Its Principles and Practices in History." Islamic Information Center. http://www.islamicinformationcentre.co.uk/dawah.htm.

Arabi, Muhyiddin Ibn. *Divine Sayings: The Mishkat al-Anwar*. Translated by Stephen Hirtenstein and Martin Notcutt. Oxford: Anqa, 2004.

Augustine. *The Literal Meaning of Genesis*. Translated and annotated by John Hammond Taylor. In *Ancient Christian Writers* vol. 1., edited by Johannes Quasten, Walter J. Burghardt, and Thomas Comerford Lawler, 41–42. New York: Newman, 1982.

Ayoub, Mahmoud. "Jesus the Son of God: A Study of the Terms Ibn and Walad in the Qur'ān and Tafsīr Tradition." In *Christian-Muslim Encounters*, edited by Yvonne Yazbeck Haddad and Wadi Zaidan Haddad, 65–81. Gainesville: University of Florida Press, 1995.

———. "Towards an Islamic Christology, II: The Death of Jesus, Reality or Delusion (a Study in the Death of Jesus in Tafsīr Literature)." *The Muslim World* 70, no. 2 (1980) 91–121.

———. "Trinity Day Lectures." *Trinity Seminary Review* 32 (Winter-Spring 2011) 7–18.

Barker, Gregory A., and Stephen E. Gregg. "Muslim Perceptions of Jesus: Key Issues." In *Jesus beyond Christianity: The Classic Texts*, edited by Gregory A. Barker and Stephen E. Gregg, 133–52. Oxford: Oxford University Press, 2010.

Bauckham, Richard, and Trevor A. Hart. *Hope against Hope: Christian Eschatology at the Turn of the Millennium*. Grand Rapids: Eerdmans, 1999.

Bebawi, George H. "Atonement and Mercy: Islam between Athanasius and Anselm." In *Atonement Today*, edited by John Goldingay, 109–22. London: SPCK, 1995.

Beehner, Lionel. "Religious Conversion and Sharia Law." Council on Foreign Relations, 2007. https://www.cfr.org/backgrounder/religious-conversion-and-sharia-law.

Bennett, Clinton. *Understanding Christian-Muslim Relations: Past and Present*. London: Continuum, 2008.

Castor, Trevor. "10 Things Muslims Believe About Sin." Zwemer Center for Muslim Studies. https://www.zwemercenter.com/guide/sin-according-to-muslims/.

Carman, John B. *Majesty and Meekness: A Comparative Study of Contrast and Harmony in the Concept of God*. Grand Rapids: Eerdmans, 1994.

Chabad.org. "Translation of the Weekday Amidah." Kehot Publication Society. http://www.chabad.org/library/article_cdo/aid/867674/jewish/Translation.htm.

Chishti, Saadia Khawar Khan. "*Fiṭra:* An Islamic Model for Humans and the Environment." In *Islam and Ecology: A Bestowed Trust*, edited by Richard C. Foltz, Frederick M. Denny, and Azizan Baharuddin, 67–82. Cambridge: Harvard University Press, 2003.

Cohon, Samuel S. *Essays in Jewish Theology*. Cincinnati: Hebrew Union College Press, 1987.

Coward, Harold. *Sacred Word and Sacred Text: Scripture in World Religions*. Maryknoll, NY: Orbis, 1988.

Cragg, Kenneth. *The Call of the Minaret*. Rev. ed. Maryknoll, NY: Orbis, 1985.

———. *Jesus and the Muslim: An Exploration*. London: Allen & Unwin, 1985.

Darwin, Charles. *The Origin of Species by Means of Natural Selection*. London: John Murray, 1860.

Deedat, Ahmed. *Crucifixion or Cruci-fiction?* Durban: Islamic Propagation Centre International, 1984.

Denny, Frederick Mathewson. "Daʿwah." In *Encyclopedia of Religion*, 2nd ed., edited by Lindsay Jones, vol. 4, 2225–26. Detroit: Macmillan Reference USA, 2005.

Esposito, John L., ed. "Furqan, al-." In *The Oxford Dictionary of Islam*. Oxford: Oxford University Press, 2003.

Francis. *Evangelii Gaudium*. Apostolic Exhortation. Vatican, November 24, 2013. https://www.vatican.va/content/francesco/en/apost_exhortations/documents/papa-francesco_esortazione-ap_20131124_evangelii-gaudium.html.

Gardet, Louis. "Allāh." In *The Encyclopedia of Islam*, edited by H. A. R. Gibb, et al. Leiden: Brill, 1979.

Greear, J. D. "Theosis and Muslim Evangelism: How the Recovery of a Patristic Understanding of Salvation Can Aid Evangelical Missionaries in the Evangelization of Islamic Peoples." PhD diss., Southeastern Baptist Theological Seminary, 2003.

Guessoum, Nidhal. *Islam's Quantum Question: Reconciling Muslim Tradition and Modern Science*. London: I. B. Tauris, 2011.

Haleem, Muhammad Abdel. "Qur'an and Hadith." In *The Cambridge Companion to Classical Islamic Theology*, edited by Tim Winter, 19–32. Cambridge: Cambridge University Press, 2008.

Hillenbrand, Carole. *Introduction to Islam: Beliefs and Practices in Historical Perspective*. London: Thames & Hudson, 2015.

Iqbal, Muzaffar. "In the Beginning: Islamic Perspectives on Cosmological Origins." *Islam and Science* 4, no. 1 (Summer 2006) 61–78.

Jacobs, Louis. *A Jewish Theology*. London: Darton, Longman and Todd, 1973.

Jewett, Paul King, and Marguerite Shuster. *Who We Are: Our Dignity as Human; A Neo-Evangelical Theology*. Grand Rapids: Eerdmans, 1996.

John of Damascus. "St. John of Damascus's Critique of Islam." Orthodox Christian Information Center, 2006. http://orthodoxinfo.com/general/stjohn_islam.aspx.

Kärkkäinen, Veli-Matti. *Creation and Humanity. A Constructive Christian Theology for the Pluralistic World*, vol. 3. Grand Rapids: Eerdmans, 2015.

———. *The End of All Things Is at Hand: A Christian Eschatology in Conversation with Science and Islam*. Eugene, OR: Cascade, 2022.

———. "Hope Gone Awry—An Odd Bed Fellowship of Islamic and Christian Neo-Apocalypticism." *Dialog: A Journal of Theology* 61, no. 1 (Spring 2022) 32–38.

———. *I Believe. Help My Unbelief!: Christian Beliefs for a Religiously Pluralistic and Secular World*. Eugene, OR: Cascade, 2024.

Kepnes, Steven. "Turn Us to You and We Shall Return: Original Sin, Atonement, and Redemption in Jewish Terms." In *Christianity in Jewish Terms*, edited by Tikva Frymer-Kensky et al., 293–319. Boulder, CO: Westview, 2000.

Khalidi, Tarif. *The Muslim Jesus: Sayings and Stories in Islamic Literature*. Cambridge: Harvard University Press, 2000.

Kogan, Michael S. *Opening the Covenant: A Jewish Theology of Christianity*. Oxford: Oxford University Press, 2008.

Kritzeck, James. "Holy Spirit in Islam." In *Perspectives on Charismatic Renewal*, edited by Edward D. O'Connor, 101–12. Notre Dame: University of Notre Dame Press, 1975.

Küng, Hans. "A Christian Response." In *Christianity and the World Religions: Paths of Dialogue with Islam, Hinduism, and Buddhism*, edited by Hans Küng, Josef van Ess, Heinrich von Stietencron, and Heinz Bechert, 109–30. New York: Doubleday, 1986.

Largen, Kristin Johnston. *Baby Krishna, Infant Christ: A Comparative Theology of Salvation*. Maryknoll, NY: Orbis, 2011.

Leirvik, Oddbjørn. *Images of Jesus Christ in Islam*. 2nd ed. New York: Continuum, 2010.

Leslie, Donald Daniel, David Flusser, Alvin J. Reines, Gershom Scholem, and Michael J. Graetz. "Redemption." In *Encyclopedia Judaica*, vol. 17, edited by Michael Berenbaum and Fred Skolnik, 151–55. 2nd ed. Detroit: Macmillan Reference USA, 2007.

Luther, Martin. *The Large Catechism of Martin Luther*. Translated by Robert H. Fischer. Philadelphia: Muhlenberg, 1959.

———. *Luther's Works*. Vol. 1, *Lectures on Genesis 1–5*. Edited by Jaroslav Pelikan and Helmut T. Lehman. Minneapolis: Fortress, 2002.

Merad, M. Ali. "Christ According to the Qur'an." *Encounter* (Rome) 69 (1980) 7–15.

Meshal, Reem A., and M. Reza Pirbhai. "Islamic Perspectives on Jesus." In *The Blackwell Companion to Jesus*, edited by Delbert Burkett, 232–49. Oxford: Wiley-Blackwell, 2011.

Metropolitan Museum of Art. "The Prophet Muhammad and the Origins of Islam." https://www.metmuseum.org/learn/educators/curriculum-resources/art-of-the-islamic-world/unit-one/the-prophet-muhammad-and-the-origins-of-islam.

Micheau, Francois. "Eastern Christianities (Eleventh to Fourteenth Century): Copts, Melkites, Nestorians, and Jacobites." In *The Cambridge History of Christianity*, 371–403. Cambridge: Cambridge University Press, 2006.

Mohamed, Yasien. *Fitrah: The Islamic Concept of Human Nature*. London: Ta-Ha, 1996.

Muhammad, Sayyid. *A Compendium of Muslim Theology and Jurisprudence*. Translated by Saifuddin Annif-Doray. Sri Lanka: A. S. Nordeen, 1963.

My Islam. "99 Names of Allah." https://myislam.org/99-names-of-allah/.

Nasr, Seyyed Hossein. *The Encounter of Man and Nature: The Spiritual Crisis in Modern Man*. Rev. ed. Chicago: Kazi, 1997.

———. "Response to Hans Küng's Paper on Christian-Muslim Dialogue." *Muslim World* 77 (1987) 96–105.

Nazir-Ali, Michael. *Frontiers in Muslim-Christian Encounter*. Oxford: Regnum, 1987.

Newby, Gordon D. "Angels" and "Jinn." In *The Oxford Encyclopedia of the Modern Islamic World*, edited by John L. Esposito. Online edition (Oxford Reference). Oxford: Oxford University Press, 2000.

Niebuhr, Reinhold. "Sin." In *A Handbook of Christian Theology*, edited by Marvin Halverson and Arthur A. Cohen, 348–51. New York: Meridian, 1958.

O'Shaughnessy, Thomas J. *The Development of the Meaning of Spirit in the Koran*. Rome: Pontifical Oriental Institute, 1953.

Özdemir, İbrahim. "Toward an Understanding of Environmental Ethics from a Qur'anic Perspective." In *Islam and Ecology: A Bestowed Trust*, edited by Richard C. Foltz, Frederick M. Denny, and Azizan Baharuddin, 3–37. Cambridge: Harvard University Press, 2003.

Parshall, Phil. *Muslim Evangelism: Contemporary Approaches to Contextualization*. Downers Grove, IL: InterVarsity, 2003.

Pathrapankal, Joseph. "Editorial." *Journal of Dharma* 33, no. 3 (1998) 299–302.

Peters, F. E. *Muhammad and the Origins of Islam*. Albany: State University of New York Press, 1994.

Pew Research Center. "Religious Differences on the Question of Evolution." February 4, 2009. https://www.pewresearch.org/religion/2009/02/04/religious-differences-on-the-question-of-evolution.

Rahman, Fazlur. *Major Themes of the Qur'an*. Chicago: University of Chicago Press, 2009.

Räisänen, Heikki. "The Portrait of Jesus in the Qur'an: Reflections of a Biblical Scholar." *The Muslim World* 70 (1980) 122–38.

Raja, Tawus. "The Spirit and the Word: Of the Command of My Lord." Al-Islam.org. https://www.al-islam.org/message-thaqalayn/vol-17-no-2-summer-2016/spirit-and-word-command-my-lord-tawus-raja/spirit-and-word.

Ravi, N. S. R. K. "A Comprehensive Listing of References to Jesus ('Isa) in the Qur'an." North American Mission Board, March 13, 2016. https://www.namb.net/apologetics/resource/a-comprehensive-listing-of-references-to-jesus-isa-in-the-qur-an/.

Roberts, Alexander, James Donaldson, et al., eds. *The Ante-Nicene Fathers: Translations of the Writings of the Fathers Down to A.D. 325*. 9 vols. Edinburgh, 1885–97. https://www.ccel.org.

Robinson, Neil. *Christ in Islam and Christianity*. New York: State University of New York Press, 1991.

Robson, James. "Aspects of the Qur'anic Doctrine of Salvation." In *Man and His Salvation: Studies in Memory of S. G. F. Brandon*, edited by Eric F. Shape and John R. Hinnels, 205–19. Oxford: Manchester University Press, 1973.

Ruzgar, Mustafa. "Chance and Providence in the Islamic Tradition." In *Abraham's Dice: Chance and Providence in the Monotheistic Traditions*, edited by Karl W. Giberson, 107–28. New York: Oxford University Press, 2016.

Samuel, Reda. "The Incarnation in Arabic Christian Theology from the Beginnings to the Mid-Eleventh Centuries." PhD tutorial, Fuller Theological Seminary, School of Intercultural Studies, 2010.

Saritoprak, Zeki. *Islam's Jesus*. Gainesville: University Press of Florida, 2014.

———. "Mary in Islam." *Oxford Bibliographies*, 2015. https://www.oxfordbibliographies.com/display/document/obo-9780195390155/obo-9780195390155-143.xml.

Schwarz, Hans. *Eschatology*. Grand Rapids: Eerdmans, 2000.

Smith, Jane Idleman. "Reflections on Aspects of Immortality in Islam." *Harvard Theological Review* 70, nos. 1–2 (January–April 1977) 85–98.

Smith, Jane Idleman, and Yvonne Yazbeck Haddad. *The Islamic Understanding of Death and Resurrection*. Albany: State University of New York Press, 1981.

Studio Arabiya Institute. "The Difference Between the Meccan and Medinan Surahs in Quran." https://www.studioarabiyainegypt.com/the-difference-between-the-meccan-and-medinan-surahs-in-quran/.

Tottoli, Roberto. "Afterlife." In *Encyclopaedia of Islam, THREE*, edited by Kate Fleet, Gudrun Krämer, Denis Matringe, John Nawas, and Everett Rowson, 39–46. Boston: Brill, 2009.

Van Huyssteen, J. Wentzel. *Alone in the World? Human Uniqueness in Science and Theology*. Grand Rapids: Eerdmans, 2006.

Vatican Council II. *Gaudium et Spes*. Vatican, December 7, 1965. https://www.vatican.va/archive/hist_councils/ii_vatican_council/documents/vat-ii_const_19651207_gaudium-et-spes_en.html.

———. *Nostra Aetate*. Vatican, October 28, 1965. https://www.vatican.va/archive/hist_councils/ii_vatican_council/documents/vat-ii_decl_19651028_nostra-aetate_en.html.

Volf, Miroslav. *Allah: A Christian Response*. New York: HarperCollins, 2011.

Vroom, Hendrik. *No Other Gods: Christian Belief in Dialogue with Buddhism, Hinduism, and Islam*. Grand Rapids: Eerdmans, 1996.

Ward, Keith. *Images of Eternity: Concepts of God in Five Religious Traditions*. London: Darton, Longman and Todd, 1987.

———. *Religion and Community*. Oxford: Oxford University Press, 1999.

Watt, William Montgomery. *Muslim-Christian Encounters: Perceptions and Misperceptions*. London: Routledge, 1991.

Woodberry, J. Dudley. "The Kingdom of God in Islam and the Gospel." In *Anabaptists Meeting Muslims: A Calling for Presence in the Way of Christ*, edited by James R. Krabill, David W. Shenk, and Linford Stutzman, 48–58. Scottdale, PA: Herald, 2005.

Zayd, Abdu-r-Rahman Abu. *Al-Ghazali on Divine Predicates and Their Properties*. Lahore, Pakistan: Sh. Muhammad Ashraf, 1970.

Zebiri, Kare. *Muslims and Christians Face to Face*. Oxford: Oneworld, 1997.

Ziadat, Adel A. *Western Science in the Arab World: The Impact of Darwinism, 1860–1930*. London: Macmillan, 1986.

Zwemer, Samuel. *The Moslem Doctrine of God*. New York: American Tract Society, 1951.

www.ingramcontent.com/pod-product-compliance
Lightning Source LLC
LaVergne TN
LVHW051003080826
845145LV00009B/2434

* 9 7 8 1 7 2 5 2 7 6 7 0 3 *